D0711514

Mary Ellen Ciganovich * www.askmaryellen.com

T. R.U.T.H.
Taking Responsibility Unleashes True Healing

By Mary Ellen Ciganovich
Foreword by Cyrus Webb

Printed with Conversations Media Group

© 2018 by Mary Ellen Ciganovich

Cover Design: DW's Simple Graphic Designs
Author Photo Credit: VR Photography

Printed in the United States of America

Mary Ellen Ciganovich * www.askmaryellen.com

SPECIAL ACKNOWLEDGEMENT

For my family and friends who have encouraged me to put my daily "Truth of the day" posts into a book- Here it is especially written for you!

Thank you for your support, love and encouragement. I am very blessed to have ALL of you in my life.

"TRUTH- Taking Responsibility Unleashes True Healing", is my gift to you, our society and the Universe.

My hope is in a small way this book will change a life and make a difference in this tumultuous world.

Sincerely with love,

Mary Ellen Ciganovich www.askmaryellen.com
askmaryellen@aol.com

FOREWARD

It has been my great honor to witness the light that is Mary Ellen Ciganovich shine over the years.

She first came to my attention with her first book and after interviewing her on my radio program and staying connected via social media we became friends.

The way she has used her platform is a reminder for all of us as to the responsibility we have while on this earth: to be of service and to let our light shine bright. Mary Ellen has done that and with this book she has given us a way to daily reflect on who we are, who we can be and how we go about getting there.

TRUTH is not just something to read. It's a prompt for us to use in our reflection and when examining who we are. That is what it has been for me, and I know it can do the same for you, if you allow it to.

Cyrus Webb, media personality/
Amazon.com Top Reviewer

Mary Ellen Ciganovich * www.askmaryellen.com

This book is dedicated to and was written for ALL people everywhere who search for TRUTH!

True healing begins within yourself when you become AWARE of your TRUTH. Before you look outside yourself for ANY kind of healing philosophy (be it medical, holistic, herbal or otherwise), you must filter your thoughts, detoxify your body and settle your soul. Because when any of these three human aspects are out

of balance- a disease (or diagnosis) will come into your system to "wake you up" and bring your attention into focus.

Taking

Responsibilty for yourself

Unleashes your

True

Healing potential

It is my wish the following pages will assist you on your journey toward wellness.

Sincerely with love,

Mary Ellen Ciganovich

Mary Ellen Ciganovich * www.askmaryellen.com

TRUTH IS!

That is simple enough.

People try to make it such a difficult quest- why?

Some people search and search their entire lives
for something- the Truth - that is right in front of
them.

This daily inspirational book is here to assist you
on your journey. Every page is a Truth. You can
accept it and learn (about yourself) or you can
decide to continue on your quest. Truth never
changes! That is what makes it "a Truth". It is a
constant.

Read, enjoy and put these principles into practice
so we can ALL come together to make our society,
our world a better place.

Sincerely with love,
Mary Ellen Ciganovich
www.askmaryellen.com

Always be true to yourself!

As you begin any new chapter in your life remember to be faithful to who you are as this will allow you to have a life of integrity and honesty. Release the hold that others' opinions have on you and it will become easier to find yourself. Follow your heart to find your place in this world. Do not allow what other people say or think to influence you. You may want to gently explain to others your actions without being defensive.

Today find your own true self by following your heart.

Enjoy the day and have fun!

Mary Ellen Ciganovich * www.askmaryellen.com

Your mission in life is to elevate your consciousness.

The desire to help everyone feel as good as YOU do about a particular product/item or service is all well and good - and possibly some people do not need or want whatever treatment or service that is making you feel so good. There is only ONE person whom you need to control and that person is YOU! Concentrate on mastering your own self. This is the only mastery of which you might be capable of achieving.

Today make it your mission to elevate your consciousness.

Enjoy the day.

Mary Ellen Ciganovich * www.askmaryellen.com

As Oprah says, "Live your most powerful life!"

You can begin this process with the "knowing" that you are pure love! Loving yourself means accepting yourself (with all of your flaws and imperfections) just the way you are NOW. You cannot give love to someone else unless you first love and accept yourself. It is not possible. You create the life that mirrors your deeper beauty. You have amazing talents and gifts that only YOU can give to our world.

Today trust and be grateful for the beautiful miracle of YOU!

Enjoy the day.

Make certain your goal realization always begins enthusiastically!

By heading towards any goal with an enthusiastic attitude you will set a positive tone for your life's journey. This will accompany you from beginning to finish. Thoughts of uncertainty and insecurity will find no space in your mind because you are looking forward in the spirit of preparedness. Have faith in yourself and trust your ability to make good decisions, whether you are facing an ordinary day or life changing choices. Your optimism and eagerness will give you energy propelling you forward. This grants you the strength to face adversity with hope in your heart.

Today feel comfortable embarking upon a journey of discovery because you are ready for anything.

Enjoy the day.

Mary Ellen Ciganovich * www.askmaryellen.com

A diamond is simply a lump of coal that has handled stress extremely well!

How do you handle stress? Do you internalize it? Do you take it out on your loved ones? No matter how you handle your stresses - you CAN make a conscious choice to handle it differently. There are definite pressures in life. All of these stresses are in our lives to teach us lessons. You may choose to tum these pressures into diamonds or allow them to fester as lumps of coal turning into cancers or other diseases. In your moments of clarity experience the desire to tum your stresses into diamonds - opportunities - rays of hope!

Today take one stress and tum it into a diamond! Enjoy the day.

Choose silence to leave you feeling vibrant and connected.

Silence can make you nervous because at times you may think you need to fill this "silent" void. Learn to immerse yourself in the strength you find in this solitude. Silence is NOT the absence of sound - it is the spaces between the notes that tum noise into beautiful music. When you listen to the absence of sound you will experience your own "well of power". There is no effort needed to make yourself still. Simply settle down - quiet your mind and unplug! During this quiet time your mind will gravitate towards the Holy Power within you. One of the best ways to experience "quiet" is to wake before the rest of the world becomes alive.

Today take at least 5 minutes to commute in silence and connect to the Universe / God!

Enjoy the day!

Mary Ellen Ciganovich * www.askmaryellen.com

Connect yourself to the Universal laws of Truth - allowing your intuition (knowings) to guide you.

It is important to realize that you are a co-creator with the Universe /God allowing this Universal energy and knowledge to flow through you to others. It is always a good feeling when others agree with you. However, you are only partially responsible for this happening. God, the Universe, is working through you to send a message to whomever you have helped. If not you - God – would send someone else to do the job!

Today connect yourself to the truth of all God's laws allowing your intuition (KNOWINGS) to guide you.

Enjoy the day.

Mary Ellen Ciganovich * www.askmaryellen.com

Allow yourself to feel supportive and supported by participating in a collaborative effort with others.

To gain support allow yourself to participate in a collaborative effort with trusted friends. This energy of a collaborative effort is like spokes on a wheel with each person's energy supporting the next.

When you work "with like minds" toward a common goal it becomes a supportive and healing process. A collaborative effort helps you to balance yourself. You will gain access to far more knowledge through not acting all by yourself!

Today make the most of your life by joining with a group allowing this energy to carry you toward your goal.

Enjoy the day.

Mary Ellen Ciganovich * www.askmaryellen.com

9

Exploring your past will help you to successfully navigate the future.

In order to fully understand where you are going (your future) - you must know where you have been. Consider all the issues you have left unexplored (in your past) and how they have hindered your efforts to evolve as an individual. Through exploring these "issues" (and learning from them) you can understand how to create a more fulfilling "life journey". Look at all your "life choices" to gain a better understanding of what makes you truly happy. This exploration will empower you to make decisions in both the present and future.

Today break out of your "old mold" and enter a new phase of life!

Enjoy the day.

Mary Ellen Ciganovich * www.askmaryellen.com

Share laughter to create a more intimate bond with others.

Sharing humor with loved ones can help you grow closer in a natural and enjoyable way. Because life is so full of pressures and challenges, laughter offers a pleasurable diversion. When you laugh with friends and family you will then associate those pleasurable emotions and memories with them. In challenging times you can smile recalling these enjoyable feelings.

Today share laughter and have fun!

Enjoy the day.

Mary Ellen Ciganovich * www.askmaryellen.com

Cast off your usual routine to increase your capacity for excitement in your life.

As you go about your daily routine spice it up by trying new ways. (Drive a new route to work or try a different type of this morning - go to a different store or try new foods) Routines do give us a sense of security and they prevent us from investigating the world expanding our intellectual boundaries. Life is more exciting when you awaken your curiosity. Your discontent with life will vanish as you immerse yourself in new activities.

Today awaken your curiosity for life- cast off your usual routine become willing to love the thrill of new adventures.

Enjoy the day.

Become assured of your abilities.

An optimistic mood will assist you to become both commanding and capable of your abilities. There is no reason you should allow inexperience or

unfamiliarity to rob you of a chance at success. When you are eager to explore or learn new activities you will be guided forward. Even if your abilities in one area do not correspond with the talents needed for a particular project - your confidence will soar every time you see any project through from start to finish. Today become eager to explore new opportunities -at home and at work - because your confidence is soaring!

Enjoy the day

See your life with newly opened optimistic eyes.

Your existence is a "pallet of potential" waiting for you to tap into it! As you courageously and open mindedly explore your world you will encounter opportunities you might otherwise have missed. Become an explorer in your life - read new philosophies, travel new places, expose yourself to the unfamiliar. Step bravely into the unknown as this can help you to break ground in your personal and professional life.

Today venture outside your comfort zone.

Enjoy the day.

Mary Ellen Ciganovich * www.askmaryellen.com

Utilize your altruistic skills to help create a stronger and safer community.

Every community needs people to be of service to those less fortunate. Although, you are busy with work and family ignite your desire to share your generosity with others. Keep the humanitarian efforts simple and low key so as not to overwhelm yourself. By being of service to even one person you become a catalyst for positive change. You are also contributing to building a better community. (Call upon others to assist you with your efforts)

Today use your altruism to help create a stronger community.

Enjoy the day.

Mary Ellen Ciganovich * www.askmaryellen.com

Confront your obligations with confidence.

When you confront your obligations with
confidence you can conquer your "fears" and move
into the next phase of personal growth. Your "fears
of failure" can stop you from moving forward.
When you confront your "fears" directly and with
confidence you will find these "misperceptions"
not to be as stressful as imagined. Now you can
move forward leaving stagnation behind.

Today realize the ambitious goals you have set for
yourself- knowing that NO challenge is
insurmountable.

Enjoy the day.

Mary Ellen Ciganovich * www.askmaryellen.com

Focus wholeheartedly on the duties before you.

Becoming grounded in the present- "NOW" moment - helps you to direct your focus toward objectives that are most important. Allow worries to flee from your mind because they have no foothold in the "NOW". You are entirely concerned with this moment and doing your best. There is no thought to the possibility of failure. Concentrate on the individual details of each project you tackle in every "NOW" moment. This will allow you to complete projects efficiently and effectively.

Today focus whole-heartedly on the duties before you.

Enjoy the day!

Mary Ellen Ciganovich * www.askmaryellen.com

Like is always drawn to like!

This Universal Truth (God's Truth) has been around since the beginning of time. You attract what you are. You will attract positive attention when you move through life projecting a positive (R.E.A.L. = really enthusiastic about life) attitude. When others know they can rely on you to "add brightness" to their lives they will be compelled to seek you out. It is your likeability that will enable you to make friends. These connections with people can have an important impact on your career and life in general.

Today express happiness in your words and deeds allowing you to attract people whose personalities are as upbeat as you are!

Enjoy the day.

18

Understand how your emotions influence your actions.

Through understanding how your emotions influence your actions you will become knowledgeable of why you make your choices. Recognize the power your emotions hold over the choices you make BEFORE you make a choice. Choose whether to follow an "emotional" choice or seek counsel from your "rational" mind! Realize how your feelings are driving you and harness this power. This will assist you with making wise choices rather than hinder your progress.

Today realize your emotions are meant to serve you rather than be served by you!

Enjoy the day.

Mary Ellen Ciganovich * www.askmaryellen.com

Opening your heart to others can be an immensely satisfying experience.

Enjoy the pleasure of sharing your ideas to those who will listen and likely reciprocate. Your openness will foster closer relationships based on mutual trust and understanding. Trust always breaks down your "walls of protection" that existed previously. An atmosphere of openness that you can create with your heart results in a shared achieved "sense of peace". Today create authentic relationships through opening your heart to others.

Enjoy the day.

An overly sensitive mood may cause you to anger or react emotionally.

Choose to respond rather than react to any situation - especially when you find yourself overly sensitive. Remain aware of your feelings staying in tune with your emotional self. Do not take what others say and do personally. This will allow you to maintain an upbeat mood regardless of how other people choose to behave. Detaching from others' behavior or opinions allows you to understand their personal negativity has nothing to do with you.

Today choose to take control of your reactions- RESPOND!

Enjoy the day.

Mary Ellen Ciganovich * www.askmaryellen.com

Your thoughts are the foundation of your actions and the building blocks of your success.

Look optimistically toward your future as visualization will help you to manifest it into being. Your thoughts are your foundation bringing blessings into your life. Affirmative thoughts attract opportunities and can propel you forward fulfilling your dreams. Your attitude for life, yourself and

others will make even the grandest dreams attainable!

Use the beauty and success you envision in your mind as a blueprint to create your reality. Distractions can not come between you and your goals when your focus is fixed on the positive.

Today regard your future optimistically and you will envision that future becoming a reality.

Enjoy the day.

Mary Ellen Ciganovich * www.askmaryellen.com

Life is about choosing, experiencing, learning and choosing again.

Never take life seriously. Life is about experiences, perceptions and misperceptions. Focus on the "now moment" - the experience. What did you learn? How did/do you feel? Did you make the world a better place? Did you take even one person's life and make it better? Even when events (things) do not turn out as expected it is a gift in disguise. You might not know this at the time - it might take years to see how God has woven His plan for you.

Today appreciate your failures and choose to learn something about yourself from the experience.

Enjoy the day.

You cannot make the most of yourself in life if you do not take risks.

By risks I am NOT speaking about risks you might take physically. I am speaking about taking risks such as 1) speaking up for yourself 2) following your passion even when it seems like your dream is unattainable or 3) having the courage to leave any situation that is not right for you. Risk calling someone to tum a painful situation into a pleasure. Risk applying for a new job with an attitude of courage. Risk going to new places and meeting new friends. Through risking you grow as a person making the most of yourself.

Today get out of your comfort zone- RISK!

Enjoy the day.

Mary Ellen Ciganovich * www.askmaryellen.com

Happiness is possible - when you CHOOSE it!

You can be happy all the time - as long as you are happy with what you already have. Happiness tends to come and go through time - as our ego allows it! With your ego out of the way happiness is yours at any moment. Sadly at times external events get in our way of happiness. Things such an illness, a death or any tragedy we see on the news are all stoppers to our happiness. This is part of the "human experience". It

is normal to be unhappy with such events. The tragic part is when you allow these events to stop your happiness for years to come.

Today choose to be happy knowing you cannot

control anyone or anything.

Enjoy the day.

Mary Ellen Ciganovich * www.askmaryellen.com

Never forget how powerful your words are.

When you make a promise it is up to you to make sure your words are sacred. People who keep their promises are regarded as people of integrity while those who do not keep their promises are regarded as people who cannot be taken seriously. Promises not kept lead to disappointment and distrust. Even promises made to yourself must be remembered and kept or your self-esteem will suffer. If it is not a possibility to keep a promise go to the person and offer an alternative - asking for forgiveness. Do the same ritual with promises you make to yourself. (Ask yourself forgiveness for a promise you no longer wish to hold onto.)

Today clear your conscience and know that you are only as good as your word.

Enjoy the day.

Mary Ellen Ciganovich * www.askmaryellen.com

26

Take time to slow down.

Rushing never gets you anywhere. In fact, it might even add to your frustrations. Slowing down allows you to breathe in all your sensations and experiences. It allows you to fully focus your attention and energies on the task at hand. Working at a slower

pace helps you to complete your work more efficiently and effectively. Slowing down gives you the opportunity to flow with your natural rhythm. Let go of the "fast forward" stress and allow your body to become grounded.

Today slow down and enjoy every moment of your life.

Enjoy the day.

Mary Ellen Ciganovich * www.askmaryellen.com

Become ready for change.

When you are really ready to change - the first step you must take - is to clear a space for that change to happen. Most people have an easier time acquiring material possessions rather than letting go of them. Just like emotional baggage it is difficult to let go of material objects that clutter your reality. You must become aware of the material possessions that no longer add value to your life. Are you holding onto a material possession because it makes you feel secure or comfortable? There is a certain amount of truth to the fact that "stuff' can make you feel good only temporarily. Recognize the emotional and material hold that possessions have on you and "let go"! This will create space for you to change! Clear out your personal space leaving only objects that bring you joy. Your energy level will soar!

Today learn to have a practical and temporary relationship to objects.

Enjoy the day.

Mary Ellen Ciganovich * www.askmaryellen.com

Everything in your life has the potential to inspire you.

Through using your imagination and creative abilities you can become inspired by any life event. Creativity and imagination allow you to think and act inventively. This will assist you in the application of all your ideas. You can add a touch of excitement or an element of bliss to any ordinary moment or project. Always remember that nothing is commonplace in nature - it is only your perception that make routine activities seem dull.

Change your perception and your routine activities will be filled with a brilliance that will inspire others and you! Today unearth the lost creative possibilities that exist in many areas of your life.

Enjoy the day.

Everyone needs to be loved!

When you want love - you must come from the "loving" place within you. It is always nice to be loved by family, friends and your significant other and first you must love yourself! No one else can love you until you love you. Your outer world mirrors how you feel about yourself. In order to love yourself, first become aware of yourself. Do you accept yourself just the way you are? Do you take an interest in others? Do you judge other people without even knowing them? Do you have false motives and assumptions that you carry through your life experiences?

Let go of ALL of these falsehoods - forgive yourself- accept yourself- the love you seek is right in front of you!

Today remember the love you want exists within yourself.

Enjoy the day.

30

Finding intimacy is as simple as opening your heart.

When you take the initiative to open your heart to your close relationships you will find a new closeness opening up between the two of you. Channel your "loving feelings" into loving words and share them with the important people in your life. Consider writing "letters of gratitude" to these special people who have played vital roles in your existence. Thank them for all the love they have given to you. When you open your heart you will find your "loving relationships" returning these sentiments to you. Today show the people you care about the love you feel.

Enjoy the day.

Mary Ellen Ciganovich * www.askmaryellen.com

Relationships between two people must have balance.

An intimate relationship between two people must have a balance of shared energy. This is one of the most beautiful qualities of any relationship. It must be a give-and-take of energy occurring between two people. Both people share the talking and the listening - giving and receiving - supporting each other equally. At times this balance will change as one person needs to have more or less attention. These cycles create the ebb and flow of the relationship. However, when the balance is one-sided the relationship becomes broken and must be fixed or ended otherwise the relationship becomes draining and unsatisfying to both parties.

Today bring balance to all your relationships or let them go! Enjoy the day.

Remember to allow your human form to grow and change in many physical ways.

At times we are so focused on our emotional and spiritual self that week tend to neglect our earthly forms. Look for opportunities to move your body. Commit yourself to any course of exercise that will help you to explore your body's potential for movement. Find physical activities you truly enjoy - your good spirits will encourage you to stick with it. Take steps to become stronger and to increase your tolerance for exertion. Find friends that will encourage you as you go through your physical activities. The successes you experience in the physical sense will inspire you to test your limits in other areas.

Today recognize the importance of regular physical exercise.

Enjoy your day.

Utilize all the unique skills and talents you have been blessed with.

You will make the most of your talents when you are not afraid to show them to the world. Many people hesitate before doing this because they have been taught it is a form of boastfulness. (Pride) Do not deprive the world of something it desperately needs - you and your talents! There is a great deal of satisfaction to be had when you use the skills you have been blessed with to the fullest extent of your ability.

Today allow yourself to receive the recognition you so greatly deserve.

Enjoy the day.

Mary Ellen Ciganovich * www.askmaryellen.com

During periods of transition allow yourself to simply-BE.

The happiness you feel after a tremendous success can at times be met with a period of downtime. (depression) During this period give yourself to simply -BE(ing) {in the quiet} You may feel unsure of what to do next with your life so pause between your achievements. This period of down time is normal and will strike everyone from time to time. Human beings are active creatures feeling best when we are working or pursuing a goal. Once a goal is met clear your thoughts before immersing yourself into another project. Take time to just-BE- with your "self' and by yourself. Connect with your priorities during this mindful transitional pause in life.

Today give yourself permission to BE!

Enjoy the day.

Mary Ellen Ciganovich * www.askmaryellen.com

35

At times allow your heart to guide your actions.

You will indirectly improve your own existence when you do your best to help other people realize their dreams. The time and resources you invest in others is always return to you as humanity changes for the better. You may only be able to help one person do one thing yet your intentions go forward inspiring others to follow in your footsteps.

Today have others' interests in mind and follow your heart - be generous!

Enjoy the day.

Mary Ellen Ciganovich * www.askmaryellen.com

Rediscover the joy of play!

Adult concerns may force you to adopt an "old mindset" leaving little room for anything that might be considered fun. Take some time to allow yourself to think childlike thoughts and behave in a light- hearted manner. That childhood innocence still exists within you. Through shifting your perspective and adopting a "playful view of life" you can see new fun opportunities for recreation. If you have kids or grandkids - find fun activities you can do along with them.

Today demonstrate that you are capable of being both responsible and youthful.

Enjoy the day.

Mary Ellen Ciganovich * www.askmaryellen.com

Become a completely integrated and balanced "Human Being" - mind, body and spirit.

You will feel more alive and authentic when you achieve balance in your mind, body and spirit. Be yourself- unafraid of how others judge you or respond to your choices. Freely express yourself while becoming respectful of other people's point of view. Do not waste time or energy concealing your true self. Rather show this "self' to the world as that is "who you are" and "what you are" here to do. Today achieve wholeness while experiencing your fully integrated "human" self.

Enjoy the day.

Take a "Leap of Faith" to accomplish anything you set out to do.

At times you may find yourself contemplating an outrageous or unattainable goal. It is during these moments, when you look over the abyss, that you should allow your Faith to carry you. Do not resist the urge to jump into a new venture. Rather have no

doubt about your life as you allow the "Universal flow of goodness" to carry you forward. A successful leap of faith requires your attention to the details. Lean on that quiet "knowing voice" of your inner self as that will guide you to your ultimate destination.

Today allow your courageous "leap of faith" to guide you in time uncharted territory.

Enjoy the day.

Mary Ellen Ciganovich * www.askmaryellen.com

Make your decisions from a "point of balance".

During your childhood experience you are taught that saying ,"yes" is right and saying ,"no" is wrong. You want to avoid conflict and criticism so you push yourself accessing all demands physically and mentally possible. Before you say "yes" to any request, remind yourself you have the ability to say, "no" ! There is nothing wrong with rejecting the request of others' in order to take care of yourself first.

Today remind yourself that you have freedom of choice say either yes or no from "a point of balance".

Enjoy the day.

Mary Ellen Ciganovich * www.askmaryellen.com

Experiences that you don't want lead you to experience what you DO want!

All of the events in your life are connected. Like a beautiful tapestry your life is woven together through all your experiences - good and bad. It is especially important to remember this as you go through times when you feel directionless or unsure of what to do. These are the times (experiences) that will lead you to a profound change in your life. Like a puzzle when all of the pieces are not there you cannot make sense of the picture.

Today remember there is always a hidden gem waiting to be discovered through your experiences - have faith!

Enjoy the day.

Release the "fear" of making wrong choices.

When you create a decisive mindset you will make progress on all your immediate goals. (make sure you also look at your bigger picture) Choose to see decisions as exciting opportunities - a way to explore a new path. Release the "fear" of making wrong choices as there are NO wrong choices just stepping stones to learning. Every decision made leads you to explore a new opportunity. Every part of your life is rewarding and valuable when you perceive it correctly.

Today correct all misperceptions allowing your "fear" of making wrong choices to fall away.

Enjoy the day!

Mary Ellen Ciganovich * www.askmaryellen.com

42

Visualize your day without judgement.

Over time you have learned to suppress some of the most fun aspects of your individuality. To rediscover and embrace these traits simply ask yourself, " what would you do if you knew no one would judge your choice?" Life is so short. You must make the most of every single second - embracing all of the good and fun things in life as well as all of life's hardships.

Today use this day to live without judgement.

Enjoy the day.

Go with the "flow of life" rather than pushing against it.

To go with the "flow of life" you must first have awareness of yourself, presence of mind and the ability to blend your energy with all other prevailing energies. Going with the flow does not mean to sit back and do nothing hoping for the best. Going with the flow means you let go of your individual agenda and listen to your "Higher Power". Tap into your core energy and flow with it - going where this energy leads allowing your resistance to fall away.

Today be open to multiple ways of achieving your goal.

Enjoy the day.

44

Assert your independence and live your life on your terms.

Asserting your independence and living life on your terms can help you to find your Truth - your purpose. You can create a life that will make you happy, fulfilled and satisfied. Listening to advice from others can be enlightening and you always need to check with your "knowings" to see if their advice will work for you. Become confident enough to make choices that empower and gratify you regardless of what others advise. By doing this I can guarantee the life you create will be the one you most desire.

Today choose to make your independent mark on the world!

Enjoy the day.

Mary Ellen Ciganovich * www.askmaryellen.com

Spend time with people whose presence you find pleasant.

When you spend time drawn to entertaining and engaging individuals you will respond with overtures of friendship. Your sense of fatigue and stress will simply melt away being replaced with energetic feelings of well-being. This enthusiasm from others is contagious and can spread through you to all you meet. Hold onto this sense of excitement as you go through your day.

Today spend some time with people whom you find pleasant to be around.

Enjoy the day.

Think differently and act differently to make changes to your usual routine.

Feel innovative today. Make changes to your usual routine by imagining a variety of scenarios that may take place. Use your mind (thoughts) to build a different pleasurable picture for your day. Now use your actions to make it happen. Develop creativity in every project you handle. Tell yourself you are capable of accomplishing any goal while using your thoughts (and actions) to challenge your ambitions. All of this resourcefulness you demonstrate is a direct result of your ability to see what you wish then act upon it.

Today be creative with your thoughts following through with your actions.

Enjoy the day.

Feel positive (R.E.A.L. = really enthusiastic about life) about your ability to achieve your goals.

Pessimistic thoughts easily become real-life roadblocks. Negative attitudes can grow to become reflected in everything you do. When you view the world optimistically it is impossible to feel helpless or out of control. A positive (R.E.A.L.) attitude inspires you to look for opportunities and take advantage of challenging personal or professional projects. Any difficulties the Universe I God puts in your path can be handled with your positive empowering attitude.

Today allow your attitude to carve a path that leads you to success.

Enjoy the day.

Mary Ellen Ciganovich * www.askmaryellen.com

48

When you focus on worry you waste your energy and time!

You may find yourself over-thinking your plans or trying to figure out exactly how to make them successful. Through doing this you are actually hindering your progress. You cannot force the Universe I God to move things into existence. Accept the spaces in life where unknowns exist – allowing the solution to present itself naturally. When you shift your attitude away from the anxiety of worry a joyful experience ensues. Your worries dissipate and solutions prevent themselves naturally.

Today accept the limitations of what you know and trust the Universe I God to fill in the blanks.

Enjoy the day.

Your work should be something that feeds your soul.

How does your work make you feel? Do something everyday that propels you forward on your "life journey".

Make a greater effort today to accomplish your duties with unswerving devotion. Show others they can trust you implicitly. Of course, not all parts of any job are fun or fulfilling- you must do as many things as possible to fill your spirit. Consider how you can change the nature of your job to closely align with your passions. If you are "stuck" in a "job" that is not fulfilling then you must find a solution (balance) before that "stuck feeling" begins to affect your health, your relationship and other areas of your life.

Today assess the value your work has in your life - look at things through a new perspective.

Enjoy the day.

When you look at other people you see yourself.

The qualities you see around you are directly related to the traits that exist in you. As I have said before, "like attracts like", is one of the most powerful Spiritual laws of the Universe! You will attract individuals into your life that mirror who you are. When you see beauty, sweetness, divinity or light in the soul of another - you are seeing the goodness that resides within you. When you see traits in others that evoke feelings of anger, annoyance or hatred you are seeing reflected back to you those parts of yourself that you have disowned or do not like. Everything is

a learning lesson - what do you still need to learn? Today as you go about your day feel gratitude for all the mirrors you see - good and bad.

Enjoy the day.

Focus on quality to make all your life experiences more meaningful.

It is not the quantity of time that matters, it is the quality of the experience during every life moment that matters. One fulfilling experience can eclipse many empty moments. Every minute is an opportunity to love yourself and others. Take quality time to develop self confidence, self respect and exhibit courage. When you focus on quality foods a modest portion will nourish and satisfy you. Also, a few hours of deep sound sleep can leave you feeling more refreshed than an entire night of interrupted sleep.

Today focus on quality rather than quantity to make all your life experiences meaningful!

Enjoy the day.

You are on Earth in a physical body because you still have things to learn.

It is through your physical form in this physical world that you can experience life and learn. In this world you know happiness, sadness, love and loneliness. You can understand the "value of life" since you have known darkness. When you are in your pure spiritual state there are no limitations of time and space - also no pain or suffering. On earth you are limited and your separation allows you to learn through love, forgiveness and compassion. Today know "you are a spiritual being having a human experience".

Enjoy the day.

Mary Ellen Ciganovich * www.askmaryellen.com

Use the "good china" every day because today is all that matters!

How many of you save your good china for company - your good clothes for Sunday or your nice jewelry for a special evening out? This is a common tendency to try to "save things" for a special occasion. You never know when your day might be your last. Let's begin to celebrate each and every day that we are alive! Use the "good china"- where are your "good clothes" and enjoy the "special" pieces of jewelry - Now!

Today celebrate life!

Enjoy the day.

When you honor others by treating them correctly you honor yourself.

The Golden Rule" - Do unto others as you would have them do unto you"- is a key concept in many philosophies, religions and spirituality texts. It is a very simple and clear cut rule. At times it is challenging to honor others when they are the ones mistreating people - yet when you honor others anyway you are holding yourself up to a higher standard. Bestowing your gift of loving kindness on all your fellow human beings will generate that "kindness" coming back to you.

Today make the world a better place by adhering to the "Golden Rule".

Enjoy the day.

Every day is a blessing and every moment of every day is full of gratitude.

There is always something to be grateful for - even when life is tough. Gratitude has a snowball effect opening your world up to many opportunities. Even during a "bad" day when you are stuck in a rut- you can be grateful at night that the day is over! Looking back at all your "life challenges" you can see the lessons you learned and the opportunities that came out of these life lessons. Rise above disappointments. Let the past mistakes go. Do not hold on or "beat yourself up"- admit- forgive and move on being grateful for these disappointments as you continue your journey. Allow courage and determination to move you forward as you feel gratitude in your heart for these "life lessons".

Today be grateful for everything - being able to see, smell, touch, hear and taste "life" - just be grateful for living!

Enjoy the day.

Mary Ellen Ciganovich * www.askmaryellen.com

56

Worry is an extension of fear.

Worry is an extension of fear and becomes a very life draining experience. Worry cannot exist without your thought that something bad might happen. Why do you have a thought about something that has not happened? Worry is a self created state of mind state of needless fear perpetuated by the news media and our society! Worry uses your imagination and so does the cure for worry. Next time you find yourself worrying - or choosing worry thoughts - use your imagination to say to yourself the best outcome for your situation. Pray! Leave it in God's hands - The Universe's hands - and let go!

Today let go of worry because you have the power to change it.

Enjoy the day.

All relationships have ups and downs - know when to hold on and when to let go.

A good relationship can have a positive impact on your life and a stressful relationship can become so draining that it affects your health. It is a fine line between knowing when to hold on and when to let go or walk away. Every relationship has ups and downs-when there are more downs for both of you be honest with yourself and let go. This can be a true act of self love for yourself and the other person.

Today remember you cannot give love to someone else until you first love yourself.

Enjoy the day.

Mary Ellen Ciganovich * www.askmaryellen.com

58

Excellence is not an act - it is a habit because we are what we repeatedly do.

If you want to change something in your life- change it for the better - try consciously doing the new "good" change for 21 days in a row. It has been proven that if you do something for 21 days in a row it becomes a habit. After 21 days you will begin doing this new habit naturally. The first few days you may have to remind yourself to do whatever it is you are working on. Then day by day it will become easier until it is second nature. Of course the first step is to become aware there is something you need to change!

Today look at yourself honestly- is there something you need to change?

Enjoy the day.

Your life is your message to the world!

All of us have the ability to live a life that will inspire the people around us. Parents can inspire their children. Employers can inspire their employees. Teachers should inspire their students and students should inspire their teachers who may be tired or exhausted from hours of paperwork. Children can inspire their parents instead of criticizing them. Employees may inspire their employers by going above and beyond their job requirements. Your life is your legacy to your family, your friends and the world around you. This world can be a better place and this process begins with each and everyone of us!

Today inspire someone by setting a good example.

Enjoy the day.

Take a break- do something that will bring you joy!

When you feel "stuck", bogged down or overwhelmed take a break and do something that will bring you joy. Joyfulness frees up of the mind. You might begin by saying a little prayer - asking God to show you what to do first or how to do it. Make yourself walk away from your desk - stretch, do some deep cleansing breaths and enjoy a cup of tea or coffee. When you feel "stuck" you must find the common joyful thing that works for you. Joyfulness will allow your mind to see things differently. Joyfulness is the positive energy force that frees up your creativity. Take a walk or go outside for a minute to look up at the sky. Be quiet and allow God to speak to you - assisting you with your perceptions.

Today practice becoming joyful - about everything!

Enjoy the day.

Pure love is genuine and does not contain "ifs" or "but's"- it simply is LOVE.

Pure love requires nothing in return. True love is felt- needing to receive nothing and wanting nothing from another. Pure love is when you simply love with no motives, no judgements and no assumptions of what will be. People who require another to do certain things, say certain things and become a certain type of person are manipulators. That is not love - it is control. True love is unconditional requiring no "ifs" or "but's".

Today become loving requiring nothing in return.

Enjoy the day!

Humor opens the heart and mind so wisdom can be absorbed.

Remember the phrase, "laughter is the best medicine". Science has proven the fact that people who laugh live long and healthy lives. You cannot be worried or miserable and laugh a hearty laugh at the same time. There is a healing story about a man who was diagnosed with cancer - he knew the healing powers of laughter so he went out and rented as many funny movies as he could. He went home and locked himself in his den watching funny movie after funny movie all weekend long. On Monday he went back to his doctor and his cancer was gone! I understand this is simply a story and when you begin to research healing techniques you find many factual stories about the healing power of laughter.

Today laugh a hearty laugh!

Enjoy the day.

Mary Ellen Ciganovich * www.askmaryellen.com

63

God is always present - at times His presence is conspicuous - at times mysterious - NEVER absent.

There have been many times in life when I wondered where God was - because I felt so alone. It was at these times - in the quiet in the aloneness - when God was most present in my life. God guides us slowly - gently showing us our errors and misjudgments. He is ALWAYS with you - in your darkest hour with outstretched arms of forgiveness or in your greatest triumph with blessings and tears of joy! You are NEVER alone for God is with you!

Today become aware of God's presence that surrounds you.

Enjoy the day.

Mary Ellen Ciganovich * www.askmaryellen.com

Just because life was that way yesterday doesn't mean it has to be that way tomorrow!

As we grow up we are taught - get up - wash your hands - eat breakfast - get ready for school - come home - do your chores go to sleep and start all over again the next day! There must be a better way to teach our children the joys of living.

Understandably there are things we must do. Find a way to exude some excitement into daily life. At the very least we can make the weekends something to look forward to. Example - we have to clean the house and after we do let's go down to the nature park and take a walk. Or - example - let's all pitch in and shovel the snow then we will go sledding! As you grow up - remember - just because your childhood was not the best doesn't mean you have to repeat it in your adult life!

Today choose to make your day different!

Enjoy the day.

Mary Ellen Ciganovich * www.askmaryellen.com

A relationship is built on the foundation you build together.

Your relationships are a reflection of you. The best way to have a relationship with someone else is to have a relationship with yourself first. What are your strengths? What are your weaknesses? All of us have something we want our egos to hide. In a relationship you cannot hide because you will see yourself in the other person. The best way to build a relationship is slowly. Have fun together- build good memories together - then allow your relationship to blossom into what God wants it to be.

Today become aware all your relationships.

Enjoy YOU and enjoy the day!

Mary Ellen Ciganovich * www.askmaryellen.com

The most painful goodbyes are the ones that are never said.

We never know from day to day what the future holds. Make sure when you leave for the day that you kiss your loved ones goodbye. Say hello with a smile every morning and give a hug and a kiss goodnight. Do not hold on to anger and forgive easily. Ask yourself," If this were the last time that I would see this person is this the way I want to leave?" Do all of this because you do not know this won't be the last time you see this person. Too many people have regrets after people are gone. Do this to create peace within yourself.

Today be sure to treat everyone with the kindness and respect you yourself would like to receive.

Enjoy the day.

Promises mean everything - and after they are broken, sorry means nothing.

"Your word is your bond" is a truth that has stood the test of time. Years ago there were no written contracts a person's word meant everything. Somewhere along with the growth of society- promises had to be written down and a person was held accountable for his "word". At times adults give promises to their children only to have something else come up and break the promise.

The adult says, "sorry" and everything is supposed to be "okay". This doesn't only happen in adult/child relationships it happens in husband/wife, employer/employee or any other type of relationship. Things do happen to change plans. Reschedule whatever it was as soon as possible. Your word should be your bond because if you cannot count on yourself to keep your word then do not expect anyone else to count on you either!

Today make sure your promises are ones you can fulfill.

Enjoy the day.

Mary Ellen Ciganovich * www.askmaryellen.com

 True knowledge exists in knowing you know nothing. (Socrates)

Every time you think you have everything figured out - God says," I don't think so", and a new trial or tribulation pops up in your life for you to handle. You must understand as a "human" you know nothing! You are simply here to learn. When you understand this simple fact you have true knowledge.

Today understand you know nothing – open yourself up to new possibilities.

Enjoy the day.

Mary Ellen Ciganovich * www.askmaryellen.com

You have to step into the abyss and have faith the ground will appear.

Most all of the great inventions, literary works and ideas for careers were born when a person was in their abyss. That dark place we all go to when we think all of our hopes, dreams and finances are exhausted. We are put in this "abyss" because this is where we are finally moldable. We are finally listening to our "knowings". Out of this abyss - our "knowings" direct us toward the great ideas that change the world for the better.

Today if you are in your "abyss" have faith – the ground is right below you!

Enjoy the day.

70

No person is a failure who is enjoying life!

Enjoying life is one of the most important things you must give yourself permission to do. You can enjoy what you are doing or you can complain about it. If you are complaining about something - change it!

Life is too short not to enjoy each and every moment of each and every day - rain or shine.

Today become a success- choose to enjoy life!

Enjoy the day.

Stretch your mind by embracing new perceptions, new ideas and new interpretations of ideas.

Use this truth daily in order to "see things differently". You have heard people say, "he/she made me feel so sad." Or "I don't know why you

always make me feel?" NO OTHER PERSON HAS THE POWER TO MAKE YOU FEEL this is a choice YOU make! You were taught by society that "other" people make you happy or sad or content or whatever. You make these choices!

Why are you giving your power away to someone else? Other people do not have the power to make you feel - happy, sad, miserable, controlled - unless you give them the power to do so!

Today use your mind to stretch taking back your power - stop giving this precious gift away to others!

Enjoy the day.

Be not afraid of going slowly, be only afraid of standing still.

We all know people who do not start projects, careers or relationships they "know" they should go forward with. People who give excuse after excuse and reason after reason for staying stuck. The truth is people would rather feel "safe" in a "bad situation" then risk beginning a new project. Most people want some kind of guarantee or safety net before beginning anything new. Are you one of these people?

Today take a risk- remember even if you are going slowly give yourself credit at least you're going in the right direction!

Enjoy the day.

73

All relationships have ups and downs - know when to hold on and when to let go.

A good relationship can have a positive impact on your life and a stressful relationship can become so draining that it affects your health. It is a fine line between knowing when to hold on and when to let go or walk away. Every relationship has ups and downs- when there are more downs for both of you be honest with yourself and let go. This can be a true act of self-love for yourself and the other person.

Today remember you cannot give love to someone else until you love yourself first.

Enjoy the day.

The longer you dwell on your misperceptions (problems) the greater the power these problems have over you!

When you dwell on your misperceptions berating yourself for your wrong-doings you give these misfortunes great power over you. So much power they happen over and over and over again. You wonder why? You must focus on the life you want to have as if it already is that way! Misperceptions - misfortunes - happen to everyone. Let them go. Learn from them. Go forward and create the wonderful life God I the Universe intends for you to live.

Today let go of all misperceptions - write them down on a piece of paper - bum it - shredded it - symbolically letting them go.

Enjoy the day.

Allow your "human form" to grow and change in many physical ways.

At times we are so focused on our emotional and spiritual self that we tend to neglect our earthly forms. Look for opportunities to move your body. Commit yourself to any course of exercise that will help you to explore your body's potential for movement. Find physical activities you truly enjoy. Your good spirits will encourage you to stick with it. Take steps to become stronger or to increase your tolerance for exertion. Find   friends that will encourage you as you go through your physical activities. The successes you experience in the physical sense will inspire you to test your limits in other areas.

Today recognize the importance of regular physical exercise.

Enjoy your day.

Utilize all the unique skills and talents you have been blessed with.

You will make the most of your talents when you are not afraid to show them to the world. Many people hesitate before doing this because we have been taught it is a form of boastfulness (Pride). Do not deprive the world of something it desperately needs - you and your talents! There is a great deal of satisfaction to be had when you use the skills you have been blessed with to the fullest extent of your ability.

Today allow yourself to receive the recognition you so greatly deserve.

Enjoy the day.

77

Allow your self-assurance to shine.

When you allow your confidence to speak for you it will free you of the need to prove yourself. If you are struggling with a lack of self-confidence you may become demanding. Through cultivating confidence, you will feel less of a need to be aggressive. Instead, your self-confidence will assist you to feel better about yourself. The better you feel about yourself the better other people will respond to your ideas, opinions and proposals.

Today let your confidence speak for you - feel good about yourself!

Enjoy the day.

Give yourself permission to receive.

Many people enjoy "giving" to another yet when it comes to "receiving "they may feel uncomfortable - as if they do not deserve it. Giving and receiving are part of the same cycle. Learn to receive as easily as you give. Allow yourself to open the "channels of Abundance" for yourself and others. Accepting a person's gift is a gift in itself. Your gratitude and sincere appreciation joins with their "energy of abundance" and nurtures all involved.

Today allow yourself to be a conduit and accept on behalf of a loving Universe/God.

Enjoy the day.

"Control Dramas" are not necessary.

Some people thrive in conflict. They are not happy unless there is "drama" playing out around them. Many people do not realize how these unconscious strategies called "Control Dramas "are used to gain power or get their way with others. "Control Dramas "are used by anyone who feels low on power and wants to manipulate another. This person will "make" you pay attention to them and elicit a reaction. They feel full filled at the expense of your feelings. Now your relationship is out of balance.

Today protect yourself from "Control Dramas".

Enjoy the day.

A great many people "think" they are listening when they are only thinking about what they going to say next to defend their views!

Become aware - are you really listening to the context and the meaning behind the words people are saying to you? Or are you watching them speak as you think about what you can say next to defend your point. People are always talking about themselves -if you REALLY want to get to know someone - LISTEN - listen to their words, their tone of voice, their expressions then you will begin to know the "true" person behind the mask!

Today beginning to really listen.

Enjoy the day.

Mary Ellen Ciganovich * www.askmaryellen.com

Too many people seek "affirmation" instead of "information". (Drew Stephenson Acts)

"Information" is simply the facts- no bias and no judgment. To accept this you must be willing to be wrong! "Affirmation" is selectively seeking the facts that "fit" your point of view - the facts that will make you right! Let us all strive to make the "information age" more about information - the FACTS and less about all of us being RIGHT!

Today seek "information" and less "affirmation".

Enjoy the day.

The good you do for yourself is temporary - the good you do for others (the world, society) will remain forever.

All of us want to leave our "mark" in this world. The best way to accomplish this is to begin doing (or keep doing) "good" for others. This does not mean that you stop taking care of yourself. Of course, you must take care of yourself first in order to be able to do good for others. Find something you love to do -something you are passionate about, then find a place in your community where you may utilize your talents. It might be something as simple as reading to young children or helping to organize a food pantry. Each of us have many special talents that we can leave with our world to make it a better place.

Today make a list of what you love to do- what are your God given talents?

Enjoy the day.

Live your life in such a way that when your children think of fairness, caring and integrity - they will think of you. (H. Jackson Brown, Jr.)

Your children are mirrors for you. They are not your possessions and they are not your best friends. God sent these precious people to you for you to teach. He also wants you to continue to learn your lessons through your children. Do not be afraid to parent. Children want and need structure this shows them that you care for them. If your children are behaving in a way that is inappropriate - look at yourself. Do you spend time on the phone gossiping with friends instead of paying attention to your children? Do you and your mate yell and fight at home?

Today take time to look at how you live your life!

Enjoy the day.

Mary Ellen Ciganovich * www.askmaryellen.com

We can easily forgive a child who is afraid of the dark; the real tragedy of life is when adults are afraid of the light! (Plato)

Many of us are stuck in patterns or illusions that we learned as children.

We learned...

Not to trust...

Be afraid of the dark...

Do not believe everything people say... Stay away from strangers...

Most of this was simply a way of our parents keeping us safe. When we become adults we must become aware that we are still in a "darkened room". We are so accustomed to the darkness that we fear the one thing that can set us free- the LIGHT!

Today come into the light- It is not easy-at first the light will hurt - at first it will be uncomfortable and it is one of the most worthwhile things you can do to achieve your peace!

Enjoy the day.

Mary Ellen Ciganovich * www.askmaryellen.com

Do not allow your circumstances to define you - circumstances are only temporary!

The circumstances into which you are born only begin your life long journey. You do not have to stay within these boundaries. As you grow you may begin to choose the "circumstances" that you want to keep in your life and the "circumstances" you wish to change. When you go through life you will find your circumstances changing - sometimes for the good and sometimes for the bad. Remember when you feel "stuck" in a certain set of circumstances it is only temporary! If YOU allow your circumstances to define you - they become who you are and may become permanent!

Today look around you-become aware of your circumstances.

Enjoy the day.

86

The only person you can let down is you!

We are taught by our society - not to let the people around us down. In Truth - the only person you can let down is yourself! The easiest way to let yourself down is to always try to make everyone else happy -because by doing and doing and doing to meet other's expectations you are sacrificing your "sense of self'. You should take care of your family and friends but NOT at the expense of yourself! If someone else feels "let down" by something you did or did not do (unless it was an error in judgement by you and you need to apologize) it is THEIR issue not yours! Today allow some time for you - don't let yourself down!

Enjoy the day.

Mary Ellen Ciganovich * www.askmaryellen.com

87

Be sure YOU are the one making the choice - do not allow anyone else to make the choice for you!

Choices should be simple when you are following your hear- (your knowings). How many times do you make choices based on what other people expect and want from you? Your choices create your life! In order to live the life you want to live - you - make the choices you want in order to make that life happen. Do not allow "the choice" to make you into something you do not want to become. Do not allow your fears to hold you back from choices you know are correct for you to make. Follow your heart (your knowings) - the correct choice is right in front of you.

Today review the choices you have made - are there any you need revise?

Enjoy the day!

Mary Ellen Ciganovich * www.askmaryellen.com

Cut out what isn't working in your life.

Choose to actively "edit" your life script. This will empower you. By knowing you have complete control over your choices - you may choose to keep what does work for you and "edit out" the choices you have made in error. You are responsible for every experience you create - every bad experience you hold on to. Begin "editing" your life by thinking about your positive and negative experiences.

Determine the parts of your life that no longer serve you and remove them. Now think of experiences that bring you happiness, joy and peace Make these a bigger part of your life.

Today "edit your life" - making room for more happiness, love and wisdom.

Enjoy the day.

Mary Ellen Ciganovich * www.askmaryellen.com

Recognize your pain and honor it by moving through it with awareness.

Pain is something you must be acknowledge. It is a Universal "wake up" call from God! The more you "sit on it" (keeping it with you) the more the "pain" becomes a part of you. By identifying the "pain" and acting toward understanding it - you can begin a healing process. You can save yourself future suffering through freeing up any energy that is tied to your pain. Empower yourself by identifying the "pain" - what feelings or emotions - are this "pain" identifying? What is the root cause? Once you identify the "pain" you can resolve to act toward healing it.

Today acknowledge and process any "pain".

Enjoy the day.

Your spiritual path is a private journey.

Every person is walking a different personal path toward awakening. Our spiritual paths will lead us to a greater understanding of ourselves. Your inner guidance (knowings) will lead you to the right doorway. A doorway that will give you a good feeling inside. As you awaken to yourself and to the life you are passionate about living you become more attuned to what is right for you.

Your passion is brought into your awareness. Other people may share with you what works for them and only you can decide what inspires you.

Today become awake, connected, fully conscious, aware and alive - begin to walk on your own private spiritual path.

Enjoy the day.

You cannot gain a sense of power in your life while remaining a victim.

"You must learn to see the world a new," Albert Einstein. This brilliant man transformed the world's understanding of the Universe. You cannot create abundance through a mind-set of poverty and you cannot gain a sense of power by identifying yourself as a victim. Find ways to step outside your understanding and see things differently. Change your perception on a situation by looking at it from another point of view. Shift your feelings from anger to compassion and forgiveness. Connect with your Higher Self for more inspired solutions.

Today open your mind to greater possibilities.

Enjoy the day.

Add variety to your life!

Do not allow yourself to get stuck in a routine - especially one that is boring. Add a touch of variety to your life. Break up the monotony by doing things differently. Complete your tasks in a different order. Eat lunch in a new place. At break time, sit under a different tree. Give yourself a treat by going on a "grown up" field trip. It doesn't matter where you go as long as you wholeheartedly enjoy yourself.

Today enjoy yourself add variety to your life by doing something differently.

Enjoy the day.

It is impossible to be thankful and grateful without also being happy.

When you are in a state of being thankful and grateful for the life you have you will find you become peaceful and happy. Thankfulness allows you to focus on the good things going on in your life. Gratefulness makes you aware of the parts of your life that bring you peace. To become truly happy – all the time - you must be at peace. To find peace you be thankful and grateful for what you already have! The next time you find yourself in a bout of depression take out a piece of paper and write down the things in your life you are thankful and grateful for. People in your life - tips you have taken - books you have read- even things like being able to see and being able to walk or talk.

Today write down all the things you are thankful and grateful for - now go through your day being happy!

Enjoy the day.

You are already perfect just the way you are - you're only misperception is the simple fact that you just don't know it yet!

You are born perfect! You are still perfect WHEN you accept yourself just the way you are. Most of us - especially if you are a woman- look in the mirror and find flaws with our weight or skin or hair etc... etc.... Your reflection in the mirror is simply that a reflection. When you love your inner self you will love the reflection! There are always things we can improve on and the best thing you can improve on is how you treat other people. Are you kind? Do you gossip?

Fix the inner self and your reflection in the mirror will improve. Not because you have changed anything - it is improving because you finally love yourself! You do not need anyone else's approval.

Today know you are perfect just the way you are!

Enjoy the day.

Great is the reward to those who help and give to others without thought of self.

Helping and giving to others is not always easy. It takes time out of your busy day and it might require you to spend some funds out of your already tight budget. When you are put in a situation to help someone - it is the right thing to do even when it turns out that someone has used you for their own motives. Stick to the fact that YOU did the right thing. They will be punished for using you - it is not for you to judge. Allow God to handle the details. Just to do the right thing and go on about your business.

When you are helping and giving to others make sure you are doing it simply because you want to help. There should be no motives on your part and no expectations of anything in return!

Today think about someone in your life that might need your assistance.

Enjoy the day.

People are not looking for the meaning of life rather people are looking for meaning in their life!

A lot of people search and search for the meaning of life. Actually you are searching for some meaning IN your life. When you have a purpose - true calling - you are at peace and you do not long for other things. Many older adults are at a loss because they have lost their purpose for getting up in the morning. Their job was their purpose! You cannot identify with what you do or when you stop doing it you lose your 'sense of self'. What you do is not who you are - just like anything you identify with is not who you are. You might identify with being "mother," "father", "husband", "wife", "grandmother" or "grandfather" be careful because all of these things these titles are temporary! You must find meaning in your life by doing what you love to do and giving to those around you.

Today find meaning in your life - what brings you the most joy and happiness when you are doing it?

Enjoy the day.

Mary Ellen Ciganovich * www.askmaryellen.com

Before beginning any kind of "good deed" look carefully at your motives!

Many people think they are doing something good for someone when in truth they are expecting something in return. For example, you buy a birthday gift for a friend's daughter just because you want to be nice. The friend's daughter never sends you a thank you note or even a thank you email. You go on and on complaining to your husband about how unmannerly this young girl is behaving. My answer to you is- if you bought your friend's daughter a gift with the "expectation" of receiving a thank you back then you shouldn't have bought the gift in the first place! There was a motive present of being a "good" person or, possibly you had a motive – although unbeknownst to you- of being held in high regard by your friend. Motives are not always made aware to you unless you first stop and think about why you are doing whatever it is you're doing.

Today become aware of your motives and whether they are good or bad.

Enjoy the day.

Mary Ellen Ciganovich * www.askmaryellen.com

Take a day just to be- just for YOU and GOD!

Take a day to hear God - feel God - sing with God and give to God a smile. This should be a day free of sadness or complaints. It should be a day of pure energy - the energy of love. Begin by feeling, - peaceful and free - allowing God's light to shine within you. Listen to your heart, your breathing as you begin to feel God's love. Taking time for this day will recharge your energy leaving you happier and able to bring a little more light to earth.

Today plan a day to just BE - with God!

Enjoy your day.

Mary Ellen Ciganovich * www.askmaryellen.com

Know what motivates you.

Whatever you are committed to is what motivates you - so what are you committed to? Are you committed to your ego - money or material possessions? Is that what motivates you or is it your soul? Do you choose peace, tranquility and truth? Most of you would like to say you are committed to both - but how can you be? The outer self craves expensive clothes, cars, etc. While your inner soul just wants love - nothing more.

When God touches your heart with unconditional love do you feel it and accept it? Who are you and what are you committed to? Maybe you can balance both - I do not know. God will respect your choice and love you forever no matter what!

Today think about what motivates you.

Enjoy the day.

Mary Ellen Ciganovich * www.askmaryellen.com

When one door closes take a moment to distance yourself.

When one door closes do not stand they're leaning against it refusing - stubbornly- to move. The door that closed provoked lost ONLY when you cannot see any other way. There is always a much bigger and better door opening right in front of you. In order to see it - distance yourself. When you distance yourself you can see the range of opportunities and possibilities that are coming to you. It is very much like the difference between looking at your house from the street versus looking at your house from a small airplane. From the street you can only see the front yet from the air you can see the front, back, roof and everything!

Today distance yourself to see all of you are many opportunities.

Enjoy the day.

Mary Ellen Ciganovich * www.askmaryellen.com

101

Take command of your life!

Feel what needs to be done in your life and more importantly - DO IT! At times life will lead you to a crossroads where you will have to make a choice. It will be a perfect crossroads with two paths. One path always leads to the light while the other – although not necessarily bad - is filled with turmoil. You may not have time to think you must make a decision. To do this practice daily by doing what needs to be done in your life NOW!

Do not put things off till tomorrow for if you do-tomorrow will never come. Take command of your life so when life leads you to a crossroads - your choice will be clear.

Enjoy the day.

102

Your key to happiness is to become awake and aware of what is really happening.

Most people stay absorbed in thoughts of the past, their   future, they're troubled life or other people's lives. Many of these thoughts just tend to get lost without adding any joy or enhancement to your life. Happiness is in your control when you focus your attention on being happy exactly where you are - NOW! Happiness is a decision you make not an emotion you feel.

Today focus your attention on what is R.E.A.L.

(Enthusiastic About Life) in this moment choose happiness, joy, peace and contentment.

Enjoy the day!

The best way to lift yourself out of sadness is to tum your attention toward helping other people.

When you feel bad - at times you might need to isolate yourself to have some downtime. An example would be a grief situation. However, the best way to get out of the "blues" is to tum your attention toward helping other people. By doing a service for someone else you will begin to find answers to your own problems (misperceptions).

You will begin to feel connected and empowered and this in tum lefts you out of your sadness.

Today tum their attention toward helping someone else.

Enjoy the day.

104

Open your eyes to let your future in!

Your future is right in front of you- right NOW at this very moment. With each and every choice you make - with every bit of energy you expel or choose NOT to expel - you are shaping your future. It always amazes me when I work with clients who are "waiting" for a future moment to suddenly appear. Make that moment happen! Make choices that will surround you with the future life you want to create. When you are undecided as to what it is you want in your life then you are "blind". You must open your eyes to let the future in - let the light in - do not be afraid because YOU can accomplish anything you want in your life.

Today let's all choose to leave the world a better

place by opening our eyes to the future and the joys we have right in front of us!

Enjoy the day.

Mary Ellen Ciganovich * www.askmaryellen.com

Minimize your fear.

Visions of the future can frighten you holding you back from accomplishing your dreams. Visualize these fears meeting them directly in your mind. Feel the emotional response these fears awaken. See yourself slaying these fears as a knight would slay a dragon. When you confront your fears directly you will discover they are only terrifying in your mind.

Today courageously confront your fears as you keep yourself safe.

Enjoy the day.

Always allow yourself to feel!

Being able to feel is one of the most precious gifts God has bestowed upon you. Many of you refuse to use it - you refuse to "feel" trying to hide how you feel. Your life experiences teach you lessons when you "feel" the truths they are teaching to you. You are what you "feel" (think about) and you are what you love to do. For your light to shine you must accept your feelings and work through them allowing yourself to face the truth.

Today allow yourself to feel and practice accepting your feelings as you share these special feelings with your loved ones.

Enjoy the day.

Mary Ellen Ciganovich * www.askmaryellen.com

Your words can never speak louder than your actions.

When you think of kindness maybe you think of some big grand gesture in order for it to count. Not so! A gentle word, a smile, or any small token of kindness can make all the difference in another person's day. It is not what you say or do it is about your intentions while performing this kindness. Encourage others, stop and really listen to what other people are saying to you.

Today think about your words BEFORE you say them!

Enjoy the day.

Mary Ellen Ciganovich * www.askmaryellen.com

108

The key to living a life full of love is to accept and allow.

Accept yourself with all of your human flaws. Allow yourself- give yourself permission - to love yourself especially with these flaws. Be compassionate with yourself and others knowing they need encouragement just as you do. Become grateful for everything in your life by spending a few moments every day thanking God for His goodness. Show appreciation to the Universe by doing things for others or giving of your time and talents. Risk being vulnerable in order to have true intimacy with another. Finally practice the art of receiving as this is just as important as giving.

Today accept and allow.

Enjoy the day.

Mary Ellen Ciganovich * www.askmaryellen.com

Knowing the difference between fear and courage is to believe anything is possible!

Begin your shift out of fear towards love by telling yourself and knowing anything is possible. Connect with others "of like minds" that will support you on your life journey. When you open your heart and mind - especially joining with others - you will discover anything and everything is a possibility.

Today know you can face adversity with dignity and integrity.

Enjoy the day.

Mary Ellen Ciganovich * www.askmaryellen.com

110

No matter what the circumstances- you are responsible for the pain you caused to another.

We all know to say," I'm sorry" when we are remorseful. You are asking to be relieved of your guilt. Does this mean you should not apologize when you do something wrong unintentionally? Of course not! You are still responsible for the pain you caused another. Men will usually say, "I'm sorry" and get on with their life where as a woman wants a person (usually the man in her life) who committed the error to say," I am sorry for (explaining and taking ownership for the error). In this way women "think" maybe it won't happen again!

Today be responsible for any pain you caused another.

Enjoy the day.

Mary Ellen Ciganovich * www.askmaryellen.com

111

A change of consciousness is necessary before you can change your outer world.

Your entire world depends on your attitude towards yourself. Romans 12: 2 says, "Be ye transformed by the renewing of your mind". These are very powerful words! Your "right mind" can assist you or you may choose to listen to the "ego mind" and allow your it to hold you back. Your outer world cannot change until you choose to change your consciousness. If you like your outer world the way it is there is nothing to change. If there is anything in your outer world that you are uncomfortable with you must first change your consciousness.

Today renew yourself through renewing your mind.

Enjoy the day.

112

Live life as an adventure!

Your life is meant to be lived as an adventure. You are supposed to be having fun while living your life! God put you here to have fun - play and learn your lessons. Begin participating in your life! Choose activities that you take pleasure in - this will prevent you becoming stagnant or bored with life. Earn your living doing what you love to do and abundance will come to you as a direct result of your joy.

Today have an adventure or start planning one!

Enjoy the day.

To judge is to think you are better than others.

Do not judge! What you see in others is a direct reflection of yourself. That might be a hard statement of truth to believe and it is one of God's greatest truths. You believe you know everything and other people do not know anything. Allow other people to learn through their mistakes while you show them love and compassion.

Today be aware of what, who and how you judge - STOP DOING IT!

Enjoy the day.

Human beings do not come to Earth to get love.
Human beings come to Earth to give love.

All human beings seek and seek for a love that is
right in front of them- inside of you! The dilemma
is that you ARE love. You cannot receive love from
another, you cannot see it in another, and you
cannot be in love with another until you totally
love yourself. Many people lead needy lives trying
to fill the emotional voids of their partners. Do not
look to others to fill your emotional wounds.
Simply embrace the love within you. Keep this love
inside your heart and distribute it throughout the
world to all the souls who cross your path. Your
greatest mission is to bring love to Earth rather
than to take love from Earth.

Today give yourself and others unconditional love.

Enjoy the day.

Mary Ellen Ciganovich * www.askmaryellen.com

115

Being happy doesn't mean everything is perfect - it means you see possibilities beyond the imperfections.

Every life has imperfections. Most of us call these "problems" - I call them "misperceptions" in our lives to teach us a lesson. You can always choose happiness when you take an "imperfection" or a "misperception" and make a conscious choice to learn from it or look at it differently. Of course life is not perfect! How many of us would even appreciate it if it were? It is an interesting fact that people notice some things when they are going wrong and take things for granted when things are going smoothly.

Today choose to be happy!

Enjoy the day.

116

Be ready to enjoy life and the company of your loved ones, family and friends!

Always be ready to share in moments of laughter and spontaneity. Share and recreational activities which leaves you feeling light-hearted with positive feelings of happiness. Celebrate life and honor yourself, your loved ones, family, friends and the universe I God. Do not allow the trials and tribulations of everyday life to hold you back from enjoying spontaneous moments of joy!

Today think about how pleased and blessed you feel when you enjoy sharing your world.

Enjoy the day.

117

Most of the society we live in is blind to the love, life and grace of Jesus Christ.

Everyone - especially those of you who regularly go to church and claim to know Christ - should live, walk and act as He would. Actually, we should all live "The Word"- His Word- as life unfolds day to day- not just on Sunday- every day! Living His (Christ's) Word is much more than quoting scripture and going to church. It is seeing the need around you and taking time for others as He would do. It is not taking anything for granted. It is also becoming aware of yourself and everything around you. Christ walked in love and taught only love.

Today take at least one hour and see if you can live by Christ's words.

Enjoy the day.

Mary Ellen Ciganovich * www.askmaryellen.com

118

The life you live should be your gift to God.

Whether you build a business or a home fill it with love, light, laughter and service. In this way your life- your business - your work - your home - Becomes your gift to God. Be sure to add compassion, caring, joy and acceptance. People will flock to work with you or be in your home because of the peace you have built.

Today make your life your gift to God.

Enjoy your day.

Mary Ellen Ciganovich * www.askmaryellen.com

The Universal force of "love" is the energy that keeps you going.

The Universal force of "love" keeps you going to complete your purpose here on Earth. At times you may feel like you won't make it through the night. Then you awaken to another day. God's law of love and grace has pulled you through. This invisible force of good guides you even when you tum away from it.

Today remember God is present with you always - day and night!

Enjoy the day.

Mary Ellen Ciganovich * www.askmaryellen.com

You are entirely responsible for the life you are living.

All matter and abundance is accessible to you on Earth. Everything is at your disposal and everything you achieve is because of you, your thought patterns and your energy system. If you are unable to achieve what you want it is either because those things are not part of your "energy" (thought) system or because you desire the things for a reason that is not in alignment with your Higher Good. You will only attract what will bring you closer to your essence of true happiness. God never denies a request from the soul when it is in alignment with your essence of true happiness (your purpose here on Earth).

Today understand that you are entirely responsible for everything that is in your life - good and bad!

Enjoy the day.

Mary Ellen Ciganovich * www.askmaryellen.com

Forgive so you can become free.

Allow all sense of negativity, resentment and victimhood to be lifted from your heart. Do not hold onto anger, hurt or resentment As you are only hurting yourself. What you withhold from another you withhold from yourself. By keeping someone in prison with your thoughts You become their jailer and have to sit at the door to keep them from escaping. You are now in prison! Free another so you can free yourself.

Today give the gift of forgiveness and release your spirit to be healed.

Enjoy the day.

You will never love unless you allow yourself to be vulnerable.

You must feel the flow of your emotions to be able to feel loved. After loving someone, and being hurt by that experience, it is easy to shut yourself down.

By turning off your emotional switch you do not have to work through the pain of the broken relationship. You "think" you can hide from this emotional pain. Not so - because until you work through whatever "emotional" pain you have hidden you will not be able to love yourself or give love to anyone else. In going through these emotional "love" pains you must keep yourself vulnerable to feeling all of the joyous love emotions yet to come.

Today become able to love (trust) yourself unconditionally by accepting any emotional pain when it emerges.

Enjoy the day.

Move out of your comfort zone.

Take a risk! Agree to follow an unknown path.
Doing the same things over and over, day after day,
will not allow you to accomplish your purpose.
Commit yourself to doing adventurous new things.
Even if it is something small like driving to explore
someplace new on the weekend! Add an element
of surprise to your life and your family's life.

Mix things up - at times it is good to have a routine
or a schedule- yet family memories are made
during the fun unexpected experiences.

Today hear life calling you and see where it leads!

Enjoy the day.

Mary Ellen Ciganovich * www.askmaryellen.com

Assist others to choose correctly by first YOU choosing correctly!

You cannot make anyone else better or worse. The only person you can "make" better or worse is yourself- through your choices. You can assist someone else and point them in the direction they should go - and you can help someone to make a correct choice. Always remember - just because you see a choice as being correct for you - it is not necessarily a correct choice for someone else. The very best way to teach other's how to make correct choices is by your "life example." In other words, live YOUR life making choices that benefit your "Higher good". When people see your life changing they will know it is possible for them as well.

Today understand when there is something you want someone to do (or act like) then YOU must do (or act) that way first!

Enjoy the day.

Mary Ellen Ciganovich * www.askmaryellen.com

The greatest power in the Universe is faith!

Faith provides you the support and insight to direct your life in ways you might never have dreamed of for yourself. Faith carries you through your hardships allowing you to leave the pain behind and grow as a person. Faith transforms your character when you learn to walk in balance during times of good and bad. Faith is your foundation. Faith frees you from your fears. Faith is something you just do, something you just accept. It is a result of finding within yourself a part of God's loving consciousness.

You will find faith in your goodness, in your heart, in your knowing, and in your soul. You cannot see faith and without it you will be forever blind!

Today understand your faith in cooperation with being grateful - encourages you to pursue your dreams.

Enjoy the day!

Mary Ellen Ciganovich * www.askmaryellen.com

Life is in a constant state of change.

This Truth can provide comfort or it can provide "anticipation stress" as you wait for your situation to change. You must become flexible - adaptable to new ways of doing things. Become a pioneer of doing and seeing things differently. Our society moves forward from outdated rules and laws through change. You might not always agree with the changes yet in order to peacefully survive in society you need to become flexible. Use your "feelings of change" to promote a cause near to your heart. Any change cannot be forced, it must be allowed to flow as it takes its place in our society or in your life.

Today choose a project close to your heart where you can make a difference.

Enjoy the day.

Be true to your beliefs - Knowings!

When you say one thing and do another - people will pick up on this behavior thinking you are indecisive or not able to be trusted. You must say and act in accordance with your truth (your beliefs - your knowings). We must all truthfully communicate our ideas to others in order to be fully understood by them. The best way to persuade others is to set an example for them to follow. You will enhance your confidence and boost your power to influence others by living in accordance with what you say, believe and know to be your truth!

Today stay true to what you believe!

Enjoy the day.

Mary Ellen Ciganovich * www.askmaryellen.com

Living a balanced life requires discipline and focus.

A disciplined attitude will assist you in meeting all of your goals - at work, at home and at school. At times this might mean you set aside an enjoyable opportunity in order to complete a project. At other times, you can discipline yourself to find inspiration through taking time off to relax with family and friends. Always listen to your knowings to understand which choice you should make. As a child you understood "discipline" to be a word you did not care to hear from your parents. As an adult you know that "discipline" simply means doing what you need to do when you have time to get the job done. In other words ," do not put off till tomorrow what you can do today"!

Today balance your life through acquiring discipline and focus.

Enjoy the day.

Harmony in relationships does not mean the absence of disagreements.

Peace is a process of balance achieved through skill and caring. In a relationship, you have the choice to disagree or ask questions or offer suggestions. Do not attempt to manipulate the situation to go your way. When your partner is not listening simply stop and wait- walk away if necessary. Approach harmony in a relationship honestly and calmly from your "Higher Self".

Today bring peace into your life by finding ways to share your world harmoniously.

Enjoy the day.

Mary Ellen Ciganovich * www.askmaryellen.com

Become free to pursue your goals.

The freedom to pursue your goals without judgement or restriction is one of the basic foundations America was built upon. Those of you in other countries should have this freedom as well. Anywhere you "love" in the world you can feel this "freedom connection" by seeking out like-minded people who you can share your journey and experiences. Through feeling supported it will make it easier for you to achieve your goals.

Today seek out like-minded people.

Enjoy the day.

131

Enjoy a sense of connecting by helping and supporting others.

By helping those close to you or assisting an organization (volunteer work) you will feel useful and supportive. When you help others you invest your energy into their well-being and also assist your own wellness. Create a life that is full, meaningful and rich through supporting and sharing your life- energy with friends. Always keep in mind these friends enrich your life as much as you enrich theirs - possibly more.

Today enjoy a sense of connecting through helping and supporting others.

Enjoy the day.

Mary Ellen Ciganovich * www.askmaryellen.com

132

Life is made up of experiences.

Every time you reject an experience because of a "fear" you are limiting yourself. It might be the fear of being judged, the fear of making a mistake or the fear of being exposed for some reason. When you do this you are cheating yourself out of experiences you need to go through in order to gain knowledge and wisdom. You will make mistakes. The world is full of them. What really matters is how you respond (not react) to those mistakes.

Today be open to new experiences in order to learn and become a wiser soul.

Enjoy the day.

133

There are NO accidents in the Universe.

Everything that happens to you - absolutely everything - whether you trip on a shoelace or a boss continuously harasses you - is there to assist you in identifying a feeling that will bring you to the awareness of who you are to become. In that moment identify the feeling. Focus on it so you can learn and let it go - stopping the accidents from happening over and over. Anytime something or someone bothers you or makes you feel uncomfortable learn from it instead of trying to sidestep the feeling.

Today understand there are no accidents!

Enjoy the day.

Mary Ellen Ciganovich * www.askmaryellen.com

Rejoice- feel the joy of being alive!

Today feel the joy of being able to choose your highest frequency to vibrate in your life. Celebrate the fact that no matter what is going on in your life - life has a good side. Even when the odds are stacked against you become determined to keep joy in your life as you pursue your worthwhile goals. Perseverance is a virtue that enables you to follow through with all of your ambitions and goals. Make sure you deal with your difficulties, delays and setbacks with hope in your heart that a better plan will unfold. The challenges you face are an inevitable part of your goal realization process.

Today keep hope in your heart and the hold on to the joy of being alive!

Enjoy your day!

Nothing is true or false -

Everything is the color of the crystal you look through.

What you perceive in your life is a reflection of a combination of your beliefs, your knowings and your experiences. Everyone knows you can either see a glass half-full or half-empty. The choice you make will be a reflection of what you have been through in your life and/or what you have been taught by society. Remember you can always choose differently.

Today be aware of the color of the crystal you look through to see your life experiences.

Enjoy the day.

Mary Ellen Ciganovich * www.askmaryellen.com

136

Lift your energy to attract love.

You will always attract what you are. When you

want to attract love you must first love yourself. You will then see in your outer world what you are in your inner world. Did you know that more than one half of the people in this world do not open their heart to love for fear of being rejected? They simply wait to be loved so they can love in return. When you feel love towards another and you feel rejection - do not stay stuck in this negative feeling. Learn from it. Learn how to love yourself. Simply focus on Love without expecting anything in return. By lifting your energy in this loving way you will end up attracting the love you desire.

Today lift up your energy to attract pure love without expectations, motives or judgments.

Enjoy the day.

Mary Ellen Ciganovich * www.askmaryellen.com

Freedom is the opportunity to do what you want when you want and the ability to choose how you want to do it.

No matter where you were born at the time of your birth - you were free and innocent. Due to geography and politics your freedoms are controlled. Even people in America who think they are free or not free if they allow there for fears to bind them. The ability to think your own thoughts and make your own choices is very precious. The price for freedom is high! Many people all over the world have given their lives in order to pursue freedom for their country and its citizens. Freedom does not give anyone the right to belittle people, hit people or hurt another. True freedom gives you the right to think your own thoughts and make your own judgements as LONG AS YOU RESPECT THE THOUGHTS AND JUDGEMENTS of other's. You do not have to agree and you must give to them the respect and freedom you want.

Today be free!

Enjoy the day!

Mary Ellen Ciganovich * www.askmaryellen.com

Your body is a sacred vessel- a vital part of your connection to your spirit.

Be in touch with how your body feels. These different sensations that are sent through your body are the essence that keeps you present every moment of your life. Your body connects your spirit to the physical world. Take special care of this physical body being attuned to the world around you as your awareness increases. Always remember your body is your temple for your "spirit" to reside in - so take care of it. Keep it clean and healthy just as God gave it to you.

Today realize your body is your temple for your spirit and by taking care of "this body" it becomes your gift to God!

Enjoy the day.

A miracle is not the suspension of a natural law but the operation of a higher law.

Miracles can be created by God and by you! A miracle occurs every time you have a change in perception and choose to see things differently. When you raise your vibrational level by focusing on the "good" you are creating a miracle. When you forget about perfection and accept yourself as perfect just the way you are - then you create a miracle.

Today create a miracle - see things differently.

Enjoy the day.

Mary Ellen Ciganovich * www.askmaryellen.com

140

Perseverance is a virtue that enables you to follow through with all your ambitions and goals.

Even when odds are against you become determined to see that your dreams are worthwhile - this is perseverance. Make sure you deal with your difficulties, delays and setbacks with hope in your heart that a better plan will unfold. The challenges are an inevitable part of your goal realization process.

Today proceed along your chosen path realizing that you are blessed to persevere.

Enjoy the day.

Mary Ellen Ciganovich * www.askmaryellen.com

Your personal power is defined through your gifts (talents)!

Use your talents to demonstrate to the world how you understand yourself and your capabilities. The world benefits when you willingly share your talents. All of us have many talents and if you are in doubt as to what your talents or gifts are ask a friend or family member. Ask yourself what do you "enjoy" doing. This can lead you towards defining your talents if you are not yet aware of them. Your earthly existence provides you with many opportunities to explore your purpose and yourself while utilizing your skills to positively touch the lives of others.

Today embrace your gifts and allow your talents to shine new light on the world.

Enjoy the day.

142

Notice the simple beauty of living - slowly!

Society teaches us to value speed and getting things done quickly. We learn that doing something quickly is more valuable than making the most of every moment. We fail to notice the simple beauty of living. You are taught that you have to rush - answer every email - return every cell phone call - immediately - and deal with overflowing schedules both at work and at home. Slow down to allow feelings of contentment and relaxation to flow through your being.

Today take advantage of opportunities to nurture yourself- take a moment to just enjoy life!

Enjoy the day.

You are born worthy - your worth is intertwined with your very being.

The concept of your self-worth is reinforced by your actions. I am not talking about self esteem - that is simply how you feel about yourself at any given moment. Your worth is not your intelligence, talent, looks, etc... Your worth is immeasurable as a child of the Universe I God. You are a special part of the Universe! Every time you appreciate yourself, treat yourself kindly, broaden your horizons or see that your own needs are met you are recognizing your value.

Today awaken to be inspired by the worth that is inside of your being.

Enjoy the day.

The key to happiness is being awake and aware of every moment.

Forget becoming absorbed in worry, thoughts about the past, the future, your life or other people. Your happiness is in control when you focus on experiencing joy, peace and contentment in the present moment. The "NOW" moment is all that exists - since the past and future are simply thoughts. Drop this "mental" world to become able to experience a depth of richness, joy and peace in this "sacred" moment of NOW.

Today whatever you are doing enjoy it – without allowing negative thoughts, fears, complaints or judgments to destroy the moment.

Enjoy the day.

Choose your own way of doing things - cultivate creativity!

Just because an idea or way of doing things is popular does not mean it is right for everyone. You must determine what is right for you. There are always many options available. Do not feel overwhelmed or pressured by family, friends or society to do anything that is not right for you. Make a decision to go against the flow of popular choices - if that is what YOU believe- choosing instead to be your own person.

Today understand you have the right to make your own choices and be respected.

Enjoy the day.

No one deserves to be subjected to feeling ignored, disrespected or shut out.

If this is happening to you the first thing to remember is that YOU are NOT to blame. Someone else is projecting their pain on you. This other person does not know how to express feelings in a healthy way. They are acting as they were taught as a child. The person is acting out of pain and fear calling for your forgiveness. Feel compassion for this person. If things continue -look at yourself to see how you might be contributing to this pattern of behaviour.

Are you an enabler - allowing this person to mistreat you? Why are you staying in a situation that is not "safe" for you? And always remember, " you teach people how to treat you".

Today speak up for yourself in a loving tone giving and getting the respect you deserve.

Enjoy the day.

Work on making your life less repetitive.

Life is an adventure and should be lived as one. Never repeat the same experiences- unless it is a fun activity the entire family enjoys. Be Innovative and creative challenging yourself to step out of your comfort zone. Creativity is a driving force in life. Is it ever a wonder why marriages become boring when you do the same thing day after day, week after week, year after year? If you cannot change things change the way you do things.

Stop at different places for coffee, go to different churches on Sunday, or simply shop at different stores.

Today become aware of the patterns that are repetitive in your life.

Enjoy the day!

Don't be afraid of your emotions - when you love someone let them know!

It is often easy to take your feelings for granted especially around people you care about the most. You assume they "KNOW" how you feel.
Remember 99% of all assumptions are false. Even when you know a kind loving relationship is in place it is still nice to hear our partners say," I love you". All of us have an abundance of love to give. It is not something you will ever run out of giving. When you are in a loving relationship you have no expectations or motives or judgements of getting something in return.

Today remember that love from the heart is always unconditional - without strings - and remember if you love someone, let them know!

Enjoy the day.

Forgiveness is heart medicine.

Forgiveness is a healing tool in your life. It is the most powerful "heart" medicine you have available. Forgiveness teaches you to release your sadness in order to find gratitude for what you have learned. Forgiveness gives you the joy and freedom of knowing you are never alone. Even when you are by yourself the power of forgiveness sends you love - the love of self-forgiveness takes you from pain, isolation and fear all the way back to knowing god.

Today know "No more fearful dreams will come, now that you rest in God".· (ACIM WB 193)

Enjoy the day.

Mary Ellen Ciganovich * www.askmaryellen.com

All thoughts are creative energy.

Prayers are thought we give out to create a desired outcome. Worry is also a thought that consumes your energy. Every thought you choose creates your experience with reality and the Universe/God. When you worry you are praying and lending energy to the creation of something you do not want! Begin to retrain your mind to focus your thoughts and energy on what you do want to bring into your life.

Today gather positive thoughts to create good in your life and the world.

Enjoy the day.

Mary Ellen Ciganovich * www.askmaryellen.com

151

Listen to what your heart and soul truly wish instead of talking yourself out of your desires and dreams.

Allow yourself to do what feels right rather than what you have to do today. If you are at a job or working there are certain things you must do - ask yourself, "How can I do _____ differently and enjoy it?"

When you hear news that delights you rejoice in it acting spontaneously. This will Infuse your life with new energy giving you a fresh perspective whether at home or at work. Allow your instincts to take over as you become closer to understanding what you really enjoy. Be in the moment sensing all the joys of the world around you.

Today bring spontaneity to your day as you experience life to the fullest.

Enjoy the day.

Mary Ellen Ciganovich * www.askmaryellen.com

152

Nature is all around you- simply become still and watch.

Season by season nature changes all around us. Both cities and packed suburbs offer wildlife nooks and crannies to explore. Animals and plants are in abundance around you. Sometimes you just have to stop, look and listen! Quit talking on your cell phone long enough to look up for a bird, an owls nest or a squirrel's nest. Take time to walk in a place where the air is fresh and clean. Nature's drama is continually playing out on window ledges where tired birds stop to rest.

Today explore different communities of animals and plants recognizing we all share the world and you are just a small part of this Grand Circle of Life!

Enjoy the day!

153

See the "good" in all by coming from that place of serenity deep inside of you.

Society teaches you to beware and be careful - finding it difficult to see the good in people, places, or situations. You can change this thought pattern by becoming grateful for everything and everyone in your life - EVEN the people or situations that upset you the most! Be quiet asking yourself to see things differently. Utilize unconditional acceptance to change the things you do not like. Go into your deeper place of "being" to "feel" the beauty and warmth of lasting change.

Today encourage yourself to look deeply into ALL things in your life to "see" the real goodness at the heart of everything.

Enjoy the day.

Mary Ellen Ciganovich * www.askmaryellen.com

Learn to be attuned to your feelings by helping others.

Giving of yourself to others is an act of loving kindness that is most useful when you are also taking care of your own needs. Learning to be attentive to your feelings while helping others allows you to act in a more conscientious way. Always notice your feelings as you take on these obligations being sure to stay aware of your own needs.

Today take time to help someone by making their life easier.

Enjoy the day.

Mary Ellen Ciganovich * www.askmaryellen.com

Your present thoughts set the path for your future life.

The only limitations you have in life are the limitations your mind creates. Change the way you think and you will change your future. Try seeing your life with endless chances for love, success and abundance. Become aware of thoughts that are NOT in alignment with these goals. Envision a future full of everything you desire.

Today concentrate on all of your limitless possibilities - NOW - make them a reality!

Enjoy the day.

156

Establish endless peace in your soul by
empowering yourself to respond rather than react
in troubling situations.

When you react to a stressful situation a feeling of
heaviness manifest in your physical self. When you
respond rather than react you are choosing
productively to tum turmoil around. This choice
helps you to inwardly direct attention to balance
yourself and restore your peace. To clear negative
energy first ground yourself. Take a deep
meditative breath as you allow yourself to balance.
Know that situations which seemed hopeless -
when viewed with fear - become manageable
when viewed through a loving perspective.

Today respond - leaving you peaceful - rather than
reacting to any challenges that are facing you.

Enjoy the day.

When you care for yourself- first - you are better able to care for others.

Putting yourself first means it may be necessary to say, "No", to someone else. This will give you some peace of mind and help you to take care of you! It is easy to put off self-care until you become exhausted or overwhelmed. Understand that taking care of yourself is neither selfish nor indulgent. You must take at least ½ hour for yourself at the beginning and end of every day - even if you just remind yourself to be quiet and breathe.

Today do something to put yourself first.

Enjoy the day.

Mary Ellen Ciganovich * www.askmaryellen.com

"I AM" is the self definition of God.

"I AM hath sent me unto you." (Exodus 3:14) In my kitchen I have a framed saying of Psalm 46: 10: "Be still and know that I am God".

I love this part of Psalm 46 because every time I read it I feel peaceful. It helps me to understand that "I AM" is infinite and we as humans are limited. We are limited by our egos, our conscious minds and our subconscious minds. Our societal teachings limit us. Our beliefs limit us while our knowings free us from these traps.

We as humans will never achieve the "I that I AM" until we transcend these earthly chains and arrive to the glorious heavens above.

Today know the "I that I AM" is watching over you.

Enjoy the day.

Encouragement is the way you show compassion to others.

God puts people in your path that need to hear what you have already learned. You can be anywhere - a drugstore - a grocery store - a party or even working when all of a sudden you are caught up in a conversation with a person who says exactly what you need to hear to be encouraged to make it through your day. The opposite might also be true. You become involved in a conversation and the person whom you are speaking to becomes encouraged by what you say to them. This is compassion - it comes from the heart and is a loving way to deal with life.

Today find someone to show compassion to by encouraging them.

Enjoy the day.

Mary Ellen Ciganovich * www.askmaryellen.com

The love you feel in your heart will allow you to make a positive difference in our world.

Your kindheartedness and compassionate attitude will attract the attention of individuals who will assist you in your personal and professional worlds. Kindness will bring you many blessings when these feelings are articulated in concrete ways. Make kindness a priority by lending support and assistance to people in need of your actions.

Today let your actions speak louder than your words!

Enjoy the day.

Mary Ellen Ciganovich * www.askmaryellen.com

161

Give yourself permission and allow yourself time to smile!

Put yourself in a good mood today by allowing yourself to smile. Life in general is much more fulfilling when you allow yourself to fully experience all of life's pleasures without paying attention to annoyances and irritations. When you are in good spirits the world around you seems to be brighter, lighter and a kinder place. Cast of negative feelings of doubt, worry or any other challenges you are facing. Give yourself permission and allow yourself time to smile - enjoy life!

Today choose to be contented, delighted and happy - smile!

Enjoy the day.

Mary Ellen Ciganovich * www.askmaryellen.com

162

You attract into your life what you believe to be true.

It is not what you want that you attract into your life- you attract what you believe to be true! In other words you attract what you are- for example- if you want other people to respect you then you must first respect yourself. A more powerful way of saying this truth is to substitute the word "know" for the word "believe". You attract what you "know" to be true. When you want someone to love you - first seek that love within yourself.

Today ask yourself- what do you know about you? What do you believe to be your truths about yourself?

Enjoy the day and have lots of fun this weekend attracting what you want, believe and know to be true into your life!

Mary Ellen Ciganovich * www.askmaryellen.com

Never let adversity overcome you- learn from it!

We all go through times of adversity. Instead of digging your heels in and refusing stubbornly to embrace it - learn from the experience. In any adverse situation the trick is how you handle it. What do you learn about yourself as you go through this adverse situation? Adversity pushes you toward your destiny. Rise above these "misperceptions" with courage to learn, stand firm and face all of life's challenges.

Today allow your adversities to help you learn!

Enjoy the day.

164

Take what God has given you and make the most of your life!

Quit making excuses! I know so many people who instead of taking responsibility for their life and creating the life they really want - will talk and talk and talk giving reason after reason to "justify" the life they are not happy living. I find it interesting to observe this type of behavior. The best thing you can do for a person like this is to simply "act" like you are listening and allow them to keep their "reasons" for their life. They must "in truth" really like it or they would choose to change it. Through your example - make the most of your life with what God has given you. This may inspire others to quit giving reasons and begin getting results!

Today - take what God has given you and make the most of creating the life you want!

Enjoy the day.

Mary Ellen Ciganovich * www.askmaryellen.com

To be healthy in mind, body and spirit you must get up and move forward into the future.

Stop living in the past- kicking yourself for what you should have done or reliving events that were hurtful. Forgive yourself in order to "Free Yourself" and move into a peaceful abundant future. It is important for you to get up with the purpose of putting energy toward moving - physically and mentally into the future. Get up and get moving - physically and emotionally finding your purpose, your passion in life. Do not sit around the house feeling sorry for yourself. This will never fix anything. You must allow your energy to move. If you do not know where to begin -just start something - anything - and you will be moved, by God, in a direction to follow.

Today get up and get going- move!

Enjoy the day.

Mary Ellen Ciganovich * www.askmaryellen.com

Forgiveness is your key to freedom.

Forgiveness is NOT an option in life. In order to be rid of bitterness, rage, anger or any form of malice you must practice forgiveness. This is your "heart medicine". Forgiveness teaches you to release your sadness and find gratitude as you learn your "life lessons". It will free you from your emotional chains and give you the joy, freedom and peace you seek. Forgiveness is the inner work you do for yourself. You cannot heal without the blessing of forgiveness. Forgiveness takes time! It does involve "letting go" of another person's errors -it more importantly involves YOU forgiving yourself!

Today be forgiving- become free!

Enjoy the day.

Look upon the situations that happen to you- good and bad - as "gifts from God".

When your life is balanced it is easy to look at things as "gifts" from heaven or blessings. The true

blessings from God come to us when we are going through our hardships. These are the times we must - through our struggles - learn about ourselves. Learn to change your perceptions and misperceptions about life. See the good things that happen to you as blessings in your life and look upon the difficult times as a "gift from God" to be turned into nuggets of gold. Your commitment to God - and your faith - will allow you to have a feeling of gratitude for all your life situations.

Today be grateful for ALL of God's gifts - it will change your energy and make you feel uplifted.

Enjoy the day.

Mary Ellen Ciganovich * www.askmaryellen.com

When the world appears dim- LAUGH!

Little children laugh a lot because they are delighted by the newness of living. In adulthood, we tend not to allow ourselves this pleasure. To change is a simple matter of making a conscious decision to laugh! You are totally capable of laughing at will. When your laughter comes from "the core" of your being it permeates every cell in your physical self. An energetic boutique of whole body laughter exercises your muscles, frees up toxins and leaves you feeling relaxed. When you laugh at life's ridiculousness- anger, stress, guilt and sadness will find no place in your being.

Today open your heart to let love in- LAUGH!

Enjoy the day.

169

You are never too old to set a new goal or dream a new dream!

At times people - especially as they age - are set in their ways. They cannot "see the forest for the trees". You are NEVER too old to set a new goal or dream a new dream! Decide to shed your boundaries that have hindered your progress. You do not need to hold on to your protective mindset - expand to your full potential! Pull apart your layer of defensiveness and allow your "boundary of self' to widen. The dreams you have kept in your consciousness can now expand into fruition. See a new goal becoming part of your thoughts. Now allow these "New thoughts" or dreams to blossom!

Today allow yourself to set a new goal and dream a new dream.

Enjoy the day.

Mary Ellen Ciganovich * www.askmaryellen.com

170

One who makes no mistakes - makes NOTHING !

Mistakes are a necessary part of your learning experience. By becoming upset when you make a mistake - you learn nothing. Your learning process begins when you can embrace your mistake and ask yourself the question," what do I need to learn from this "mistake experience"? It does no good to become upset with any mistake you make or a mistake anyone else makes. It still happened. The mistake will not vanish - so learn from it! Take responsibility for your mistake - make amends if necessary and go forward. When you do not learn from your error you make the same mistake over and over again repeating the experience.

Today learn from your mistakes!

Enjoy the day.

Mary Ellen Ciganovich * www.askmaryellen.com

Within yourself are ways to encourage yourself to persevere.

Inside each of us is a power called "intuition". I call it "our knowings". This is your personal "God-given" power that encourages you to persevere through times of trouble. The ways in which you diligently approach your tasks could make you feel dependable and trustworthy. Knowing that others can rely on you just because you have the ability and the desire to complete everything you set out to do will put you in a good mood. Become responsible consider the outcome of your work so you can inspire not only yourself but others. Completing your tasks in a way that makes you proud feeds your spirit.

Today treat yourself gently and with care so you can connect with your knowings and alleviate stress. Enjoy the day.

Remember, if you are headed in the wrong direction- God allows U-tums!

Do not waste your life going in the wrong direction - staying in a bad relationship or putting up with a boring job. When you find yourself going in the wrong direction make a U-tum and find your true path. Plan to go back to school and get proper credentials or if it is a bad relationship plan the most loving way to end it. You might need to stay in the job/relationship while you plan for the future. Always remember to be as truthful as you can with an employer or your partner so they may also plan ahead.

Today make sure you are going in the right direction!

Enjoy the day.

Always make sure you see everything, overlook a lot and correct a little.

This Truth of the day applies to all people - parents, employers, employees and ordinary people running day-to-day errands. As you go about your day overlook many of the little errors that occur around you. See everything by setting a good example to those you meet - especially your children and correct only occasionally as this is the way you would like to be treated.

Today practice this truth- use your awareness to see everything - overlook a lot of everyone's small errors and correct only a little.

Enjoy the day!

We are all sinners, for we are all missing the mark - the mark is to become awake and aware of yourself.

You must awaken - become aware - to your thoughts, your words and your actions. Your world will respond to your thoughts and to your actions when you wake up. To become awake means to become aware of yourself. The easiest way to become aware of yourself is through how you view others. Do you judge them? Are you critical? Do you spread gossip? We all fall short at times and when we become aware of our own shortcomings we can become more compassionate towards others.

Today look at yourself and understand how you can see others differently - wake up to you own shortcomings!

Enjoy the day.

Mary Ellen Ciganovich * www.askmaryellen.com

175

True stillness comes from moments of solitude when you allow your mind to settle.

There is no effort required to still yourself. Simply settle down and allow the frantic activities from your day to dissipate from your mind. While quiet your mind will gravitate toward the Holy Power within you. Even muddy water will become clear if allowed to stand undisturbed. In the same way your mind will become clear when allowed to be still.

Today allow your mind to settle - find moments of solitude.

Enjoy the day.

Mary Ellen Ciganovich * www.askmaryellen.com

Wherever you go the love of God goes with you.

Because you are love - composed by love - created out of love-love goes with you into the world. God's love is expressed through you as - the Holy Spirit - the very embodiment of Divine love.

Anything not loving must be forgiven as there is no other choice.

Today and always - know the "love of God" goes with you wherever you go.

Enjoy the day as you spread God's Love!

Fear is met and destroyed with courage and love!

The opposite of love is fear. Just as David had courage to slay the Giant Goliath - you can slay your fears with your courage! First you need to become aware of the fears you hold on to. Next you must sweep them from your mind eliminating ALL "fear thoughts". Any fears you hold onto will come to pass as you are giving them power.

Now gather all of your "loving thoughts" to use as ammunition and with courage confront your fears. In this miracle moment your fears will evaporate just like the illusions they have always been!

Today meet and destroy one of your fears!

Enjoy the day.

Your suffering results from your refusal to accept and bless your life just the way it is - right NOW!

How many of you try to fix- yourself - your relationship - your friends - your family or any other part of your life? Stop finding fault with your life and start taking part in your life. Enjoy it! Inhabit your life fully with energy, integrity and purpose. Stay present in your life as there is nothing lacking or broken in your life. These parts are misperceptions and must be seen as lessons needing to be learned. Your life is perfect just the way it is!

Today stay in the "NOW" moment knowing your life is perfect just the way it is!

Enjoy the day!

Heaven is a place of peace within our hearts and minds.

Whenever you are at peace- you are in "Heaven". We all know "Heaven" as the place we aspire to go to when we "cross-over". You can find "Heaven" at any moment of any day when you choose to find peace. Quiet your mind uplift your heart to find a piece of "Heaven" right here on earth. Find your "state of grace" (piece of Heaven) that exists inside all of us. Grace is your inner beauty radiating outward, touching everyone you meet.

Today becomes quiet and find your own place of peace- your "state of grace"- your own "Heaven".

Enjoy the day.

Mary Ellen Ciganovich * www.askmaryellen.com

180

Never put money before your spouse or your children.

"The most important things in life cannot be bought - they are felt with the heart". This paraphrase is one of my favorite quotes. Money is a good thing and a necessity but it must be kept in perspective. Spending time with your spouse, your children, your family and your friends should be the most important aspects of your life. Motivate yourself to become grateful and abundance will flow easily into your life.

Today spend time with your spouse and your children- Be sure to UN-PLUG!

Enjoy the day.

181

Change what does not work in your life!

When you do not change what is not working in your life you will continually have the same issues day after day. Small changes can have a big effect. Sweeping changes - changing a lot - may put you into a tailspin of turmoil. Take one small step- change one thing in your life that does not work for you.

Changing one thing can eventually change everything. Just do not stay stuck! Have faith and risk! Your life will always tum out for the better.

Today change something - however small- that is NOT working in your life.

Enjoy the day.

182

Remember without opposition or resistance there is no potential for progress.

This is a basic physics principle. An eagle can't fly without air - a ship cannot sail without the resistance of the water and help from the wind. We cannot walk without the power of gravity. The next time you face opposition or resistance in your life know it is a sign you are making progress. Do not resist - do not swim against the waves -just allow. What you resist persists until you learn and let go.

Today let go of any resistance in your life and allow your life to flow.

Enjoy the day.

Mary Ellen Ciganovich * www.askmaryellen.com

Just be in the - Here and Now - in the moment.

Time alone is a gift. Being by yourself and taking care of YOU is a healthy way to access what is going on in your life. Having this kind of quiet in your life allows you to decompress from our hectic world. You can sort through your perceptions and your misperceptions. This will allow you to strengthen your ability to interact with others in a positive, energizing way.

Today nurture yourself to become a positive force in the world.

Enjoy the day.

Declare your blessings -A blessing is not a blessing until it is spoken or written.

You can think about a blessing and until the blessing is actually spoken the energy of the blessing cannot be unleashed to do the good intended. You can think "good thoughts" as what you think is important. Yet simply thinking "good thoughts" will not bring them into being. You can say "good thoughts" as the spoken word is powerful - yet when you write your blessings these blessings have even more energy. Blessings- like a "good thought"- stay locked in your "house of unawareness" until unleashed.

Today declare your blessings to give them energy.

Enjoy the day.

God's time is not our time!

God has perfect timing. When God wants something to happen nothing can stop it. Your knowings will connect you to your "God advice". Assisting you to make the choices necessary to help you prepare your way.

Sit back, visualize the life you want - put all of your energies (choices) toward creating that life and allow God to lead the way.

Today understand that God's time is perfect time!

Enjoy the day.

You do not have freedom- if you are not free to be yourself.

Is there an authority figure watching over you? Do you try to be an authority figure to someone else? Of course, children must have guides and employees must have direction. These are not the situations of which I speak. It does not matter where you live if you are not free to be yourself then you are not free at all. Many people "think" they are free yet they live by controlling others or through being controlled by others.

Today ask yourself," do you have freedom to be yourself?"

Enjoy the day.

The "Law of Attraction"- like attracts like-
influences all energy.

Your thoughts are what make you - YOU! These
undistracted positive thoughts create a powerful
magnet drawing similar energy into your
vibrational field. The longer you hold any positive -
R.E.A.L.* - thought in your mind the stronger and
more powerful your energy becomes. Makes
choices according to the opportunities that will
naturally come your way by holding in your mind-
field these positive thoughts.

Today understand your thoughts have power and
your emotions (choices) bring them to life.

Enjoy the day.

*(R.E.A.L. = Enthusiastic About Life)

Mary Ellen Ciganovich * www.askmaryellen.com

188

Your journey to find a relationship is a journey to find yourself!

All of your life experiences and wisdoms are incorporated in your journey to find a balanced relationship. Your relationships -all of them - are a reflection of YOU. Define your "ideals" of what you seek in a relationship - write them down - speak them out loud. Now, YOU become these ideals - (through the choices you make and the energies you expand) and your relationship will magically appear before you.

Today write down and speak the ideals you seek in another.

Enjoy the day.

Mary Ellen Ciganovich * www.askmaryellen.com

Look for experiences in your daily life that can aide you in your growth and learning.

Explore new ways of thinking. Look for new kinds of books or take an online (free) course in something that interests you. Work on making your life less repetitive. Life is an adventure and should be lived as one as these life experiences have much to teach you. Become aware of the opportunities for growth that exist right in front of you! Doing this continuously will help you feel more alert, alive and interested in life. Try not to repeat the same experience - unless it is an activity you enjoy. (By experience I mean going places - not activities of necessity such as exercise) Be innovative and creative challenging yourself and your family. Creativity is a positive driving force in life!

Today learn from your experiences and choose to see each moment as an opportunity to absorb knowledge and ideas.

Enjoy the day!

190

The enthusiasm you exude while living your life will inspire others.

We all have a need to share our thoughts and feelings. As you communicate your ideas you will discover the people you share with are just as enthusiastic about your ideas as you are. Allow these friends to see the full intensity of your excitement! This "excitement" acts as fuel to propel your ideas into becoming realities. People will want to join with you in promoting your ideas toward becoming Real!

Today Let Your Enthusiasm influence your communication skills.

Enjoy the day.

191

Focus on the positive nature of the people in your life.

An idealistic attitude can assist you to see the positive potential in people. At times we discount people and circumstances that fail to meet our expectations. Learning to look for and distinguish positive potential will enable you to tum disappointments into blessings. Adjusting your expectations takes awareness and practice as we have been taught since birth to have expectations, motives and judgements about everything and everyone in our lives. Your attitude can also help you to see situations differently.

Today recognize the people you love as the individuals they are and your circumstances as changeable.

Enjoy the day.

Mary Ellen Ciganovich * www.askmaryellen.com

192

Choose to keep a calm, centered mindset in all your activities.

You will feel focused and enhance your productivity when you choose to keep a calm, centered mind. In this way you will be able to meet your responsibilities as you succeed in all your tasks. You can enhance this effectiveness by choosing to take breaks to release any built-up tensions. (Try deep breathing exercises) Clear your mind of scattered thoughts staying calm to allow focused thoughts into your mind.

Today focus on your work successfully and efficiently accomplishing all tasks.

Enjoy the day.

Mary Ellen Ciganovich * www.askmaryellen.com

193

Release thoughts of doubt!

When you release "thoughts of doubt" you can create an opening for optimism and excitement. This new energy will provide you with limitless opportunities every day. By choosing to consciously release doubts-you are opening your mind to all of the endless possibilities that exist in your life. This results in feelings of optimism, inspiration and excitement propelling you forward to take immediate action on your opportunities.

Today consciously release all doubts from your mind.

Enjoy the day.

Mary Ellen Ciganovich * www.askmaryellen.com

True power comes from within.

Success does not come from other people or external situations- true power (success) comes from within you! You can respectfully guide others when you respect them - and you cannot respect them until you respect yourself. An effective leader treats everyone as his/her equal - who listens to ideas from those in his/her guidance. (This truth applies to family, friends and work situations.) It is important to treat everyone around you with the same kindness you want to receive. A compassionate leader with quiet strength inspires people to trust and follow.

Today remember true power comes from within.

Enjoy the day!

Accept your "human fallibility".

Because we forget that people are imperfect we tend to hold others' to impossibly high standards - even higher than we ourselves are demonstrating to the world. Become willing to give second chances. Love people despite their mistakes. This will become a testament to your ability to recognize an individual's value. A compassionate and realistic approach will ensure that others treat you with the same kind-hearted tolerance you show to them. When you are forgiving and tolerant of others' mistakes - you demonstrate your awareness and acceptance of your own human fallibility.

Today interact with others by graciously accepting their faults, errors and idiosyncrasies.

Enjoy the day.

Mary Ellen Ciganovich * www.askmaryellen.com

Spend time alone to release confusing emotions.

When you are experiencing a tumult of confusing emotions being alone can help you deal with these feelings. It can be difficult to focus on confusing emotions when faced with the demands of work and everyday life. Through being alone and finding stillness you can comfortably access your deepest and emotional issues. No one will judge your feelings or interrupt your search for peace.

You can quietly reflect upon your past (or whatever these emotions are bringing up for you) while staying in the NOW moment! Through this stillness practice reach revelations about your future.

Today spend time alone to explore your inner self.

Enjoy the day.

Reconnect with your loved ones on an emotional level.

With the passage of time your relationships (family and otherwise) can become distant. Make an effort to rebuild these relationships demonstrating your commitment to the people you care about. Your loved ones should respond with warmth and similar gestures of affection. These actions will restore the closeness you want enjoyed. Some relationships may be as strong as ever just in need of a little nourishment. Also some family/friend relationships - once broken - might never be mended without first an act of forgiveness.

You can always try - just make sure you do not allow their garbage to become your own. If you are like me - you have enough garbage of your own without taking on more!

Today connect with the people who matter most to you.

Enjoy the day.

Mary Ellen Ciganovich * www.askmaryellen.com

198

Strengthen your communication skills.

At times you may become so enthusiastic in your interactions with others that you speak before you understand the full meaning of their message to you. This results in misunderstandings! Take time to clarify your communication skills so you can become better able to clearly express your ideas.

Become a better listener. To truly listen you must stop assuming what you "think" someone is saying to you! Fully stop - listen to their words - and respond with an appropriate comment. This will encourage a deeper exchange of thoughts and ideas.

Today engage in lively and productive communication.

Enjoy the day.

Mary Ellen Ciganovich * www.askmaryellen.com

199

Entertainment, amusements and fun are just as vital to your quality of life as air, food and water!

Activities and hobbies you pursue are ways to add pure pleasure to your life. This reminds you there is more to life than obligations and routine work. Much of what you do everyday is motivated by your need to survive - money - food - clothing - shelter etc... This is all good and must be a priority - yet the hobbies you indulge in are actually tools to help you build a more fulfilling life existence. These activities broaden your boundaries of experience and actively manage boredom!

Today engage in pursuits that give you joy.

Enjoy the day and have fun!

Mary Ellen Ciganovich * www.askmaryellen.com

200

Learn to detach from your possessions.

When you become tight-fisted about your material resources you increase the amount of fear you hold about potential scarcity or lost. Appreciate what you have - letting go of what is not of use to you anymore. This will make it easier for you to see the ebb and flow of your life. Allow yourself to enjoy the fruits of your labor instead of guarding against your concerns of loss.

Today find a greater appreciation for all you possess in life - let go of what is no longer of use to you.

Enjoy the day.

Mary Ellen Ciganovich * www.askmaryellen.com

Envision the results of your actions.

We all need a sense of purpose in our work and in our daily lives. At times we become so engrossed in our duties that it is easy to lose sight of the results. We might become bored thinking we are doing mostly routine tasks. Picture your work as an essential part of the human picture. See ways in which the pieces you create fit into your overall picture and true purpose in life.

Today bring your spirit into your responsibilities - move forward toward a greater path of enlightenment.

Enjoy the day.

Mary Ellen Ciganovich * www.askmaryellen.com

You cannot gain a sense of power in your life while remaining a victim!

"You must learn to see the world anew," ~ Albert Einstein.

This brilliant man transformed the world's understanding of the Universe. You cannot create abundance through a mindset of poverty and you cannot gain a sense of power by identifying yourself as a victim. Find ways to step outside your understandings and see things differently. Change your perception or misperceptions on a situation and look at your life from another point of view. shift your feelings from anger to compassion to forgiveness. Connect with your Higher Self to find inspired solutions.

Today open your mind to greater possibilities - guide your life in a new direction.

Enjoy the day.

Mary Ellen Ciganovich * www.askmaryellen.com

203

Become an inspiration to others while making your own dreams come true.

We can Inspire and motivate others by being "Our Best Selves". Just as we look at others with admiration- others look at us in the same way. Always make an effort to do your best and create a level of success.

Remember that just because you do not see yourself as a success - a younger person who admires you might see you as a tremendous success! This attitude will serve as a motivator for others who are just beginning their Journey. Demonstrate all possibilities to another - showing them how to succeed. This will allow you to become confident and fearless (if you are not already) when it comes to achieving your own goals.

Today be an inspiration to others while making your own dreams come true!

Enjoy the day.

Mary Ellen Ciganovich * www.askmaryellen.com

Let confidence fuel your efforts.

Combine a positive (REAL), focused mindset with your confidence level when taking action to pursue your goals and dreams. Your efforts will be greatly enhanced through devoting a strong focus to your goals. Just like a car must have a steering wheel to drive the power of the engine, your ambitions need focus to carry you forward toward completion. A strong sense of confidence will allow you to be successful in every undertaking!

Today allow your confidence and motivation to carry you forward.

Enjoy the day.

Mary Ellen Ciganovich * www.askmaryellen.com

205

Take Time to think about what you really need.

When you feel the need to be extravagant - ask yourself what else is going on in your life? Do you feel lack in some area of your life and this is why you must be extravagant - to make you feel better about yourself? As you uncover the motives for your spending you may find there are few things you really require. Realize that spending excessively is a way to fill any type of emptiness. Finding comfort in material goods is a way to give solace to yourself yet you will still feel the emptiness.

By understanding what is driving your needs, you will become aware of the issues in your life that require your attention.

Today give yourself a gift far richer than anything you could purchase- Unconditional love ofyourself.

Enjoy the day.

Mary Ellen Ciganovich * www.askmaryellen.com

Re-evaluate your long-term goals.

Give yourself clarity and insight to adjust your plans by reevaluating your long-term goals. As you grow in confidence and wisdom the course of your life will also grow and change. Your long-term goals will need to be adaptable to these life changes.

Periodically set aside time to reevaluate your goals to see where improvements or adjustments might be made.

Today, with your new confidence and outlook on life, breathe newness into your goals.

Enjoy the day.

207

Strengthen your level of inner harmony – Stay Balanced!

When you infuse your actions with measured constraint you can increase your effectiveness while preserving a peaceful state of mind. You will make the most of your ambition by tempering it with moderation - thus staying in a balanced state. You will be able to accomplish more while not wearing yourself out. Also, your efforts will be much more focused when you feel mental clarity and physically sharp.

Make choices that will balance your eagerness with moderation giving you focus and bringing you peace of mind.

Today take your time and enjoy the journey rather than rushing to the finish line.

Enjoy the day.

Mary Ellen Ciganovich * www.askmaryellen.com

Consciously replace all doubts and fears with positive (R.E.A.L.) statements to inspire you.

It is easy to forget that we have full control over our fearful thoughts. You have been taught to choose to see your "fears" as unproductive beliefs. Regardless of any challenges you may face you will gain strength through turning these fearful thoughts around. Replace your negative beliefs with R.E.A.L. (Enthusiastic About Life) thoughts and empowering statements. This will empower you to become stronger and more proactive toward your goals.

Today focus your energy on the achievement of R.E.A.L. (Enthusiastic About Life) thoughts to produce the results you want.

Enjoy the day.

209

Assess where you want to go in life.

Focus your talents on being successful in a way that will be meaningful for you. Reflect on what you truly want in your life - not what somebody else wants you to do, become etc...! This will allow you to find healthier ways to achieve your goals. Your confidence, ambition and motivation will lead you to become successful in your life. When you think about the direction you should take you will gain an understanding of where you should put your energy to achieve these dreams.

Today direct your attention to the things, ideas and goals that are important to you!

Enjoy the day.

Mary Ellen Ciganovich * www.askmaryellen.com

Start your day well!

From the moment you feel yourself awakening to a new day make choices to prepare yourself for a prosperous, peaceful day. When you are still drowsy and " hit the ground running" your worldly obligations make you feel fatigued and overwhelmed. On the other hand, when you have a relaxing morning - it will energize you and give you what you need to meet all your daily challenges. Begin a morning routine to help you stay focused and centered throughout the day. A gentle, reflective morning prepares you to create a conscious and thoughtful day.

Today set the tone for your day by choosing your mood - respond to circumstances with a good attitude.

Enjoy the day.

Mary Ellen Ciganovich * www.askmaryellen.com

211

Honor your feelings - feel them without judgement or action.

When you feel "fed up" with humanity take a moment to settle yourself using your "awareness of self" to contemplate what you need to learn from these feelings. There are always situations (and people) that will leave you feeling as if you humanity is going in the wrong direction. It is natural to feel let down and disappointed when you see your fellow humans acting in ways that are violent, uncaring and greedy. There are also ways for you to process your disappointment without sinking into depression. Consider all the ways you might help the situation. How can you and a group of friends do something to make a difference?

Today honor your feelings by feeling them fully - without judgement- then let them go.

Enjoy the day.

Mary Ellen Ciganovich * www.askmaryellen.com

212

Never deny others the opportunity to get to know the real and terrific you!

The fear that other people will perceive you a certain way may lead you to overcompensate by acting in a way that is not the "real" you. Accept yourself! Allow others to see you as the smart, capable, real person you are - flaws and all. The simple fact that you are willing to be yourself will help you to make a positive first impression on all you meet.

Today be who you were meant to be and shout out to the world," I am proud of the person I have become!"

Enjoy the day.

213

Open yourself up to your "Cycle of Abundance!"

Be willing to share your possessions with others. Feel generous when you see a person who has a need you can fulfill. This decision will open your world to your, "Cycle of Abundance" and prosperity. When you give to others of your possessions or treasures - you open spaces in your world to be filled with abundance.

When you hold back or hold onto your things you restrict the flow of abundance because you are acting out of fear.

Today become a light in your world - give to others.

Enjoy the day.

Mary Ellen Ciganovich * www.askmaryellen.com

Make and Take time to be alone!

The stress of being with others- at work or at play - can make you realize how much you need to take time to be alone and regroup. When you are emotionally drained - moody - spending time alone in quiet reflection can give you the energy you need to complete your day. Sit in meditation (5 minutes is all you need) simply watching your thoughts and feelings as they arise and pass. You may notice feelings of discomfort or habitual thoughts that come and go into your mind. This unease does not necessarily come from being with others. It may be your sensitivity to their thoughts and energies.

Today observe your thoughts and become aware of the affect these thoughts have on you.

Enjoy the day by observing your thoughts, let them go!

Mary Ellen Ciganovich * www.askmaryellen.com

215

Realize - change is the only constant in life.

Everything is in a state of change. Your sense of security will be enhanced when you understand this important truth. Relationships come and go. Worries and fears dissipate as you understand their lack of importance. The more you try to hold on to anything- relationship material things etc... the more you push them away. You are actually creating exactly what you don't want! For a human being in a state of change is uncomfortable -and yet that is how we learn. There is always a God-given rainbow at the end of your "change tunnel".

Today let go and let God - understanding change will give you a certain sense of peace when you embrace it.

Enjoy the day.

Mary Ellen Ciganovich * www.askmaryellen.com

Envision the results of your actions.

We all need a sense of purpose whether in our work or our daily lives. At times we become so engrossed in our duties that it is easy to lose sight of the results. We might become bored thinking we are doing mostly routine tasks. Picture your work as an essential part of the human picture. See ways in which the pieces you create fit into your overall picture and true purpose in life.

Today bring your spirit into your responsibilities - move forward toward a greater path of enlightenment.

Enjoy the day.

Mary Ellen Ciganovich * www.askmaryellen.com

When your world appears dim- LAUGH!

Laughter has always been a part of the human system of expression- even before the "art of speech" was created. Laughter allows you to connect with people you do not know. It allows you to enjoy positive shared experiences with strangers as well as loved ones. Even if you are alone by yourself, laughter has a ton of benefits. It exercises the muscles in your face and lungs while your mind assists your body to feel relaxed and content. You can shift your focus from irritability to tranquility through laughter. Laughter will open your heart to allow your "love light" in - allowing you to change your perspective and focus on what is positive in your life.

Today allow laughter to resonate through your heart filling all the empty spaces with joy.

Enjoy the day.

Release your worries and embrace a calm state of mind.

Choosing to release your worries will improve your level of efficiency and complete your work with less frustration. Rather than allowing yourself to become frustrated you can choose to control your thoughts creating a calm mindset. This will ease the sense of pressure you feel with your work thus improving your efficiency and also your productivity.

Today choose to adopt a calm focused mind in order to release feelings of anxiety and complete your tasks efficiently.

Enjoy the day.

Appreciate your life with a renewed awareness of gratitude.

Many messages you encounter during your day make you have thoughts about what you don't have rather than the abundance you do have. This leaves your gratitude level in perpetual conflict with your desire for more! Take inventory of your life's blessings. Do you own a car, have an education, own a home, or live in a clean apartment? Do you nourish your body and mind, feed your family, have a job or easily move your body?

These are all blessings because for many people throughout the world these represent great challenges. Become grateful for ALL your comforts and conveniences.

Today allow your gratitude to flood your heart realizing your abundance.

Enjoy the day!

220

Appreciate people for who they are!

You must understand the basic concept that we each benefit others in a very real way. Therefore, it is important to appreciate people for who they are with no judgments, motives or expectations. When I see a situation I do not understand I think to myself- that person is doing the best they can in this particular moment of this day. Then I say a prayer for him or her. It is important for all of us to strengthen the bonds that connect us to one another friend or family. Being able to show your concern for one another is one of our greatest joys in life!

Today provide your loved ones with assistance to show appreciation.

Enjoy the day.

Mary Ellen Ciganovich * www.askmaryellen.com

221

Focus on all the abundance you have in your life.

Choosing to focus on the abundance you have in your life can lift your mood and calm your anxiety. It will also set the creative process in motion to attract even greater levels of prosperity. Always tum yourself in a positive (R.E.A.L.-Really Enthusiastic About Life) direction sending the Universe/God a very clear message of what you want to create in your life. A new positive (R. E. A. L.) outlook will make you feel happier beginning to attract more joy and abundance into your life.

Today choose a positive mindset that will reflect a better way of living for you.

Enjoy the day.

Mary Ellen Ciganovich * www.askmaryellen.com

222

Your potential is as boundless as your dreams!

You can always visit a brighter future in your mind's eye- your dreams. Imaginations are limitless! You are free to picture a wide variety of possibilities even when your life isn't working. The longing in your heart - your knowings - will become your guide toward visualizing the goals you want to achieve.

Today allow your imagination to guide you toward a brighter future.

Enjoy the day.

Express happiness in all you do.

When you spread cheer among the people closest to you- you share the full presence of your positive (R.E.A.L. = enthusiastic about life) energy to be projected through your mood. This in tum inspires others to participate in this "atmosphere of happiness". Also, your smile and laughter will encourage the people around you to change their somber disposition. Not everyone will enjoy your gregarious nature and the atmosphere around others will be changed for the better.

Today brighten other's moods with your "smiles of happiness".

Enjoy the day.

224

Free yourself from anxiety.

In order to free yourself from anxiety remain calm and bring your attention back to the present moment. When you actively remain present in the "NOW"- there is no room or use for worry about the future. Concentrating on the "NOW" gives you the chance to see things as they really are. When you are clearly focused your anxiety will become a defeated enemy.

Today remain calm and in the "NOW".

Enjoy the day.

Mary Ellen Ciganovich * www.askmaryellen.com

225

Always know there are positive benefits to every activity you pursue.

Focus on the positive (R.E.A.L. = enthusiastic about life) benefits of all the activities you are engaged in during the day. Choose to focus on the beneficial ways your efforts help others. This will enable you to reinforce a deeper sense of meaning even in mundane activities. No matter what you are working on- your job- serving others through volunteer charities or simply caring for your family - know you doing your part to make the world a better place.

Today gain a sense of usefulness in knowing everything you do is helping our world!

Enjoy the day.

Mary Ellen Ciganovich * www.askmaryellen.com

226

Balance your world with time spent caring for
yourself.

You can remain calm and willing to see things
differently when you balance your workload with
time spent caring for yourself. When you indulge in
personal time you will renew and revive your
energy. Now you can tackle all of your
responsibilities with greater efficiency. In tum you
will feel a sense of accomplishment for the tasks
completed. Your productivity will allow you to
appreciate the time you do make for yourself.

Today balance your responsibilities with activities
you plan for yourself.

Enjoy the day and have lots of fun accomplishing a
lot while enjoying some personal time!

227

Friends act as mirrors reflecting ourselves back to us.

Friends offer you the opportunity to know yourself and grow as a person. The good you see in a friend are the good qualities you yourself possess. The qualities in a friend (relationship) that irritate you are God's way (The Universe's way) of showing you what you must learn about yourself. When something about another person or situation really irritates you and you can't let it go - then there is something about that "error in judgment" YOU must learn. By acting as mirrors friends help you to define who you are by reflecting yourself back to you.

Today be grateful for all your friends - accept them as they are!

Enjoy the day.

Mary Ellen Ciganovich * www.askmaryellen.com

Become a "Beacon of Reassurance" who others can approach for guidance.

Whether as emotional support, practical assistance or a listening ear - let other people know you are there to offer assistance. Your compassion will free them from facing their hardships alone. It will also help you in facing your own challenges. Understanding other people's struggles functions as a catalyst inspiring trust between all concerned.

Today connect with people on a deeper level - become a "Beacon of Hope" for everyone you touch.

Enjoy the day.

Utilize innovative thinking to respond to "problem" situations.

Your past experiences have taught you - you are capable of employing your strengths wisely. Your many talents when used "to see things differently" can help you cope with adversity. To successfully overcome the challenges before you use your cleverness as a tool. Always utilize your imagination and willingness to "think outside the box" to respond to any misperception (problem) you perceive.

Today use Innovative thinking to work during your day.

Enjoy the day.

Mary Ellen Ciganovich * www.askmaryellen.com

Spend time opening your mind to new ideas.

Engage in creative activities so you can strengthen your mental clarity allowing yourself to receive powerful insights. Step out of your comfort zone to take time to stretch your imagination. When you go through a trying time listen to your "Higher Self". This will awaken you to your "new innovative" wisdom that you already possess and will make you feel clearer about your goals.

By opening yourself up to new ideas you will access the insight and knowledge you need to achieve success.

Today spend time opening your mind to new ideas and new activities. Enjoy the day!

Reflecting upon your thoughts and feelings will assist you to make correct decisions.

When you begin to feel overwhelmed by a decision you are trying to make take a moment to explore your thoughts and feelings around the situation. A period of "quiet reflection" can help you get in touch with your wisdom. You will always know - in your knowings - the right choice to make. All you have to do is to STOP and LISTEN to your "inner guidance".

Today examine your feelings and explore your indecisiveness.

Enjoy the day.

232

Stay true to yourself because there are only a few people who will always be true to you.

The only person that can ever truly take care of you is you! The first person you should get to know is yourself! If you do not know you then why should other people get to know you? When you know yourself and you like yourself you are never alone or lonely.

Today get to know your likes and dislikes so you can stay true to yourself.

Enjoy the day.

Mary Ellen Ciganovich * www.askmaryellen.com

233

Let go of having to understand WHY?

The "Why" something happens does not matter. Everything happens for a reason that is beyond your comprehension level. You do not need to know the "Why". When you are conscious and AWARE of your life - you regard your experiences as teachers learning from every lesson as they appear on your path. The answer you seek as to "why" something happened - may come later or never at all. Simply thank the experience - be grateful for it and let it go.

Today become aware of letting go of "Why"!

Enjoy the day.

Mary Ellen Ciganovich * www.askmaryellen.com

Do not carry the "weight of the world" upon your shoulders.

Guilt is when you take responsibility for other people's choices and for the type of life those choices attract. This often causes you to carry the "weight of the world". The "weight" of all those people whom you want to save and ·"believe" you can save. The "weight" of all things you wish were different because their issues trigger things in you that you must work on yourself. This "weight" you carry on your back is called guilt. Then you wonder why your back hurts or your neck, shoulders or head! You can take responsibility for only two things - #1 the choices you make in your life and #2 the way your life is at this moment! Nothing else!

Today cleanse your guilt and give yourself permission to fly.

Enjoy the day.

Through straightforward conversation you can protect yourself from harm.

Often we fear what we do not understand. Misgivings and judgements regarding others are simply the result of the fact that you perceive these individuals differently. Follow your knowings and you will always be told when you are in harm's way. Get to know acquaintances and colleagues so they seem less threatening and more trusting. Be willing to open a dialogue with others and they will feel less threatened by you. First rule is to be SAFE - then allow your guard to come down and express your curiosity.

Today practice straightforward conversation with others.

Enjoy the day.

236

Exhibit patience toward all people - especially the people you care about!

"Love is patient, love is kind", (1st Corinthians). During any time of year - change of seasons especially -   you may feel temperamental and reactive toward people whom you do not meet your expectations. Through being candid with your conversations, responding through kindness and patiently accepting people's differences you can appreciate your loved ones as the unique individuals they are in the world. As you appreciate your family, friends and coworkers your relationships will grow stronger and deeper.

Respond - do not react - with tolerance rather than emotionally or judgmentally.

Today express non-judgmental love for family, friends and coworkers.

Enjoy the day.

God works in such a way that you are always at the right place at the right time.

The Universe I God works so you are always at the "right place" at the "right time". You may not feel this way as "things" might not always fall into alignment with YOUR vision. You cannot see the entire picture. Remind yourself that God (and the Universe) orchestrates life to be in perfect balance. When you miss an appointment and feel down - You just are not supposed to be there. Train yourself to see God/ The Universe as always supporting you.

You can create your experiences (perceptions) with your interpretation of how God is supporting you.

Today feel lucky and see how God coordinates your perfect timing.

Enjoy the day.

238

Take a deep breath and respond- never react!

When you feel sensitive to a situation you might find yourself over reacting instead of responding to the issue. Take a step back before you ruin a new relationship and utilize your deep breathing techniques to respond - whether at home or at work. Respond from a Higher Place within yourself. This may take some practice especially if you have

learned to react! In the long run it will save many hurt feelings and reduce the unnecessary drama in your life. Before you interact with anyone - remind yourself to take a deep breath and RESPOND! Today feel more centered and calm as you face the day.

Enjoy the day!

Keep your thoughts and your physical space organized.

Create a more organized and comfortable environment in which to handle your personal and professional tasks. Become inspired to create organized spaces and beautify your personal space. Through doing these simple tasks you will also be creating mental order. Sort through your possessions and get rid of things that do not add value to your life experience. Release what no longer serves you or pass along to family and friends things they might enjoy. By keeping both your thoughts and your physical space organized you can be assured that you can handle any challenge life gives you.

Today become organized and teach your children to be organized also!

Enjoy the day.

240

Take pride in your accomplishments by choosing not to compete with others.

At times you may feel that you are not accomplishing as much as you should or as much as those around you. Tell yourself that what others do matters less - what YOU do matters most! How you feel about your progress is what really matters as you challenge yourself to greater achievements. Once you stop competing or comparing yourself with others you will have more energy to devote to your obligations.

Today choose not to compete - take greater pride in your accomplishments.

Enjoy the day.

Mary Ellen Ciganovich * www.askmaryellen.com

241

Adopt an entirely new mode of thinking or being - become a lifelong learner!

When you are restless and life choices seem difficult for you - it may be time to adopt a new way of thinking. How? First become a "lifelong learner" willing to explore new horizons and opportunities. Stop holding yourself back through your boring routines. Read a book about a foreign land, converse with people whose philosophies are different from yours or immerse yourself in past - times (hobbies) you have never tried. Your mind will open with each new experience you incorporate into your "bank of wisdom". This will allow you to begin to think differently seeing the world in a new way.

Today challenge your mental self- become a lifelong learner!

Enjoy the day.

Let go of your defense mechanisms- become honest with yourself.

When you have to defend something - someone says or does to you - then there is a truth you still need to learn from that person, relationship or situation. Shakespeare wrote, "Thou dost protest to much!"- meaning you never have to defend the truth. Truth just is - it is not difficult or hard to understand. You have defense mechanisms you have developed over time. These behaviors you repeat are the ones that have worked for you. As a Spiritual being you have the ability to rise above these habits to see the truth right in front of you. Become honest with yourself. What do you truly want in life? You can then connect your desires with the creative power of the Universe/God.

Quit making excuses and being defensive about why you are not living the life you want. Change your habits!

Today be honest with yourself!

Enjoy the day.

Mary Ellen Ciganovich * www.askmaryellen.com

Overcome the fear of being alone.

Silence can be extremely powerful. In the silence Life/God can speak to you. Your solitary time is vital to your health and well-being. Many people feel like they are not living unless they are surrounded by noise and activity. Do not confuse "being alone" with "being lonely". Many people in relationships are very lonely. Before you can have a good relationship you must love and accept "being alone" with yourself. If you do not like being alone with you why should anyone else want to be with you!

Today enjoy spending some time alone.

Enjoy the day.

Mary Ellen Ciganovich * www.askmaryellen.com

Leaning how to trust means knowing what trust is.

In order to have trust you must first experience trust. When you were growing up if you had care givers (parents or family members) who said one thing with "words" yet their actions were totally different - you grew up not knowing trust. Now as an adult you can look back at certain situations - forgive - and go forward. You can choose to repeat the same patterns you grew up with or you can choose to get rid of doubt (creating trust) by first matching your words with your actions. Make yourself a perfect example of "trust" in your family and in your life. In this way the cycle is broken and "Trust" will begin to flourish.

Today make sure your words match your actions - building trust in yourself.

Enjoy the day.

Mary Ellen Ciganovich * www.askmaryellen.com

Connect to your core by teaching and living only LOVE!

You cannot teach your children "love" when you do not live in a loving atmosphere. Living in "love" means living with no judgments, expectations or motives. Living in "love" means admiring the beauty and diversity in everyone around you. When you walk through a forest you admire all the trees not just the oaks or the pines. All of us are connected and all of us are equal - that is a simplified version of what Christ came to teach us. Treat ALL people of ALL religions, races and creeds with the respect they deserve. By living your life this way, you will connect to your core teaching "unconditional love" to your children.

Today connect to your Higher Self and teach only "love".

Enjoy the day.

246

You attract the attention of like-minded individuals.

If you are self-confident and at peace with yourself you will attract others who are also self-confident and at peace. If you are needy and down on life then you will attract other people who are also down or depressed in their life. Don't quell your happiness to avoid offending others. Share your happiness with others by inviting them to appreciate your gladness and upbeat nature.

Today concentrate on making people happy - in this way you can give the world around you a wonderful gift!

Enjoy the day.

Spend quality time in the company of people you care about the most.

The time you spend with the people you care about most will be rewarding and reassuring. Even a few minutes in their presence can add something very special to your day. Appreciate all they have done for you. Allow them to inspire warmth in your heart and know you are worthy of their love.

Today socialize with people you care about the most- even if it is just by phone. (no email – you need to hear their voice!)

Enjoy the day.

Mary Ellen Ciganovich * www.askmaryellen.com

248

Life is a collage of beginnings and endings.

All of your beginnings and endings run together to form the portrait of your life. Yet before you can begin a new chapter you must achieve a feeling of closure with the last one. Without this sense of closure you cannot see the importance of the lesson you are learning. This closing act or transition assists you with letting go of your past misperceptions.

Today honor your experiences - past or present – let go of feelings of anger or uncertainty seeking closure.

Enjoy the day.

249

Prove your trustworthiness by honoring your confidences and promises.

Look back at your personal history and see if you have ever let your friends or family members down by betraying their confidences. You can always ask forgiveness - apologizing for your error. Go forward avoiding any similar mistake in the future. Gossip is far away from God and your true spiritual path.

Today prove yourself worthy of trust by allowing your actions to match your words.

Enjoy the day.

Mary Ellen Ciganovich * www.askmaryellen.com

To see TRUTH you must look without prejudice, expectations, motives or judgments.

You will never understand anything - truth or otherwise - while you hold opinions, assumptions and judgments about other people. Allow all of these to fall away - then you may begin to see truth. When you do begin to see others clearly you will be surprised how peaceful your life becomes! Truth is simple - it simply is TRUTH. You can teach your children and other people in society truth by the example of how you live your life. You cannot profess "Truth" and live a life of lies or deceit. The Universe/God will tum your lies or deceit around and throw them right back at you.

Today look at everyone without prejudice, assumptions, expectations or motives.

Enjoy the day!

Mary Ellen Ciganovich * www.askmaryellen.com

251

You are always on your "right path"!

No one knows better than you what your "right path" for your life is. Sometimes people think they need someone else such as a counselor or a therapist to make sure they are on their "right path". Counselors and therapists have their place in our society and in your "knowings" you can feel your "right path". Someone once said," a counselor is someone who borrows your watch to tell you what time it is." They are simply reinforcing for you what you already know.

Parents can and should have input for your "right path" just make sure they are not steering you toward a path they wish they had followed. You are the only person who must live with and be happy with the path you choose.

Today understand whatever choice you make is correct for you!

Enjoy the day!

Mary Ellen Ciganovich * www.askmaryellen.com

The greatest teacher you can ever have in life is experience!

The more "life experiences " you have AND have learned from - the deeper your "wisdom well" becomes. People who have learned from their experiences become peaceful. They understand the Universal principles or God's principles that govern all of us. As you grow in wisdom you understand concepts like, "worrying about anything will not fix or change it" and "what you focus on expands - what you continually think about will happen."

Today become aware of all your life experiences and be grateful for the lessons you have learned. Enjoy the day!

Allow yourself to focus on the pure joy of simply being alive!

Your home should be the place where you feel secure, at ease and relaxed. Do not allow worldly concerns to intrude upon your tranquility at home. Establish your peace by putting thoughts of the past or the future away and live in the moment.

When you do this you will discover more joys to be had in simply existing. Learn to maintain a blissful emotional equilibrium that comes from within you when you make choices NOT to become affected by outside circumstances. Day by day this contentment will grow as you through become grateful for simply being alive!

Today awaken to your inner tranquility.

Enjoy the day.

Mary Ellen Ciganovich * www.askmaryellen.com

Expand your vision for your life.

When you expand your vision the circumstances (situations) you need to fulfill your destiny will follow. You can create more potential for your plans to grow and evolve. Often people become so attached to the "vision" that when they reach their goals they actually are limiting their potential for further abundance. Expand your vision - inviting even more ideas, plans, and opportunities to begin in your life! Set aside some time to be alone - relaxing into a meditative state - bringing to your mind more goals thus allowing you to achieve even more successes!

Today expand your vision for your life.

Enjoy the day.

255

Find tangible ways to express kindness and compassion toward others.

Express compassion to other people through supportive activities. These activities will increase your own sense of satisfaction. When you reach out to share your kindness in tangible ways you are able to see the results from your efforts. Possibly you can volunteer to assist a charity. You might find an elderly person whom you can help by assisting at a grocery store. You might find a younger person who could use your adult guidance. There are so many opportunities around you to make a positive difference in our society!

Today gain a sense of fulfillment from your ability to show kindness and compassion in tangible ways toward other people.

Enjoy the day.

Recognize opportunities as they arise.

Feelings of optimism flow through you when you engage in new opportunities. When you move through life with your head buried in work seldom realizing a new opportunity is at hand you become blind to these advantages. You begin seeing them as obstacles disguised by your fears. Take time to regularly scan your horizons for opportunities - new prospects or projects. Grab these experiences as they come before you. There are merits to every opportunity that presents itself. Create the optimum future that is within your very reach through seizing new opportunities!

Today learn to seize and see every opportunity. Remember you can create them yourself!

Enjoy the day.

Mary Ellen Ciganovich * www.askmaryellen.com

Build a more intimate relationship with the people you care about.

The individuals you are "intimate" with know you in depth. Intimacy means "in - to - me - see " . Yet

many of us do not allow our loved ones to see into or behind our masks. You will feel more connected to the people you care about when you allow them to see into you! Take time with your loved ones to see into them. This connection will lead to a deeper relationship. Declare your feelings for them either vocal or written. Discovering your willingness to share your feelings allows you to share that "intimacy" with those you care about. Remember before you can see "into" anyone else you must be able to "see" yourself!

Today nourish and nurture your relationships - begin with yourself!

Enjoy the day.

Establish a solid foundation of "SELF".

When you establish a solid foundation of "self-balance" you will feel good dealing with obligations. You will enjoy a feeling of safety that comes from your stability. To create this sense of "self" it is important to focus on your goals. Take time to review your responsibilities and let go of all unnecessary ones. When you deny creating this "sense of self" you create apprehensive experiences that can knock you off balance. Crafting a stable life style ensures that a safety net will be under you allowing you to climb to greater heights.

Today create a strong foundation of "self balance" to ensure a successful future.

Enjoy the day!

Focus on your responsibilities and personal projects.

Today arrive at a level of maturity that will allow you to focus with whole hearted attention on your tasks. Put a routine in place to help you fulfill your obligations while still leaving time for pleasure.

This routine will guide you through life to help you use your energy efficiently. Be sure to take time for yourself while focusing on your projects. Assess all of your responsibilities to determine how to optimize your time. A routine will help you to abolish chaos and uncertainty.

Today adopt a routine to complete your tasks with energy to spare.

Enjoy the day.

Mary Ellen Ciganovich * www.askmaryellen.com

Enhance your productivity.

By taking time to quiet your mind and renew your focus you will enhance your productivity. Your motivated mind-set will allow you to stay focused, busy and productive. A calmed mind can release your stress. Empty your mind of all thoughts and focus on "nothingness". Repeat a calming mantra for several minutes to relax your thoughts. You might enjoy a quiet park-like setting to refresh your mind and keep your thoughts focused. These frequent periods of meditation contribute to a clear mind and increased productivity.

Today enhance your productivity by taking time to quiet your mind and focus.

Enjoy the day.

Give to others without any expectations of anything in return.

Become inspired to lend your support to family and friends. See the burdens shared by others and give a helping hand through difficult times. This will strengthen the bonds between you and your loved ones. Always give your gestures in the spirit of love expecting nothing in return. If you feel resentful because of a lack of appreciation from others, then - do not do anything for them- in the first place! Focus on letting every good deed be its own reward. This will inspire you to feel joyful about your actions.

Today make a positive difference in the world by giving to another without any expectations!

Enjoy the day.

262

The attention you pay others will make your world brighter!

When you are feeling upbeat and happy you will find yourself looking for ways to delight the people around you. Allow your compliments to emerge naturally- honestly. Through doing this you are demonstrating esteem and respect for them .
When you compliment the people you encounter - take time to admire the outcome. And always remember - the good you see in others is "the good that is also inside of YOU"!

Today take pleasure while you place an "unexpected note of positivity" into another's life.

Enjoy the day.

Mary Ellen Ciganovich * www.askmaryellen.com

263

Take time to exercise today!

Exercise will help release the tension in both body and mind keeping you more present in life. The anxiety in your mind is relieved as the tension in your body is drained away. Utilize your body's muscles to reconnect with the earth and ground yourself. Life- giving oxygen will flood your body's systems giving you the strength you need to overcome your worries. The intensity of your emotions will flow away as you become lost in your physical movements.

Today gain a feeling of serenity through taking time to exercise.

Enjoy the day!

Mary Ellen Ciganovich * www.askmaryellen.com

264

You can help others today by drawing upon your inner well of compassion.

Compassion enables you to look non-judgmentally upon the lives of those less fortunate. There is no shame in needing help- all of us have at one time or another. You have the ability to express sympathy as well as empathy in the form of action. Examine the numerous blessings you enjoy and think of ways you might use your talents to aid others.

Today strive to do all you can to ensure someone else's basic needs are met.

Enjoy the day.

Mary Ellen Ciganovich * www.askmaryellen.com

265

All people are equal in the eyes of God.

Everyone receives the same amount of love, goodwill, tolerance, forgiveness, opportunities, happiness, spirituality, healing, etc... from God. The difference between people are the choices each person makes taking advantage of their gifts from God. Some people use their gifts wisely while some people hoard their gifts trying not to let go of them (as if they will run out?) and others throw their gifts away with both hands. When you choose to see and accept your gifts you are closer to God. These people God will motivate and bless. For those who reject their gifts a sadness will befall them as well as fears, inaction and depression until they finally choose His Light.

Today be thankful for the people who allow the Earth's energy to gain greater awareness - make sure you are one of them!

Enjoy the day.

Mary Ellen Ciganovich * www.askmaryellen.com

266

Accept that bouts of dispiritedness are God's Way of telling you to relax and recharge.

A low mood may plague you today preventing you from addressing your lengthy list of holiday duties. You may feel discouraged or irritated by worldly distractions. Relief can be found in the gentle embrace of solitude. You may be dealing with a case of exhaustion from personal responsibilities. In order to regain balance simplify your activities allowing you to regain a relaxed state of being.

Today unwind and regain your energy before resuming activities.

Enjoy the day.

Mary Ellen Ciganovich * www.askmaryellen.com

267

Choices should be simple when you follow your heart.

Choices should be simple when you are following your heart. How many times do we make "choices" based on what other people expect or want from us? Your "choices" create your life! In order to live the life you want to live - YOU - must make the "choices" you need- to make your life happen. Do not allow "the choice" to make YOU into something you do not want to become. Do not allow your "fears" to hold you back from making the "choice" you know is the correct choice for you to make.

Follow your heart - the correct choice is right in front of you.

Today review the choices you have made - and learn!

Enjoy the day!

Mary Ellen Ciganovich * www.askmaryellen.com

268

HOPE - a most powerful little word and will sustain you through your many misperceptions in life.

When you have HOPE you live today planning for an even better tomorrow. You spend quality time loving your family and appreciating your friends. You will utilize humor to help you see things differently. You will set goals and always say, "I CAN"! The most important facet of your life that will steer you towards HOPE is to BE AT PEACE WITH GOD - PRAY OFTEN!

Today be at peace and pray- keep your hope alive! Enjoy the day.

Mary Ellen Ciganovich * www.askmaryellen.com

269

When you are dealing with people you dislike - it is your opportunity to learn about you.

Most of us wish we could exist in harmony with the people around us. This is only possible when you embrace the rough traits in others as being traits in you that you must correct. When you judge other people's beliefs, opinions, mannerisms etc... you are only judging yourself. Allow the individuals around you to peacefully coexist with you by showing them the same empathy and compassion you would appreciate receiving.

Today control your feelings and minimize other individuals impact on your life.

Enjoy the day.

Mary Ellen Ciganovich * www.askmaryellen.com

When you are deeply in touch with God - You can see God in everyone.

Jesus saw God in everyone. This is the reason He was such a good teacher. He did not exclude anyone. He went to the lepers, the prostitutes, the rich and the poor. He did not judge - had no motives and made no assumptions. When you have a close relationship with God you will then be able to see this "goodness" within everyone.

Today become aware of how deeply in touch with God you are.

Enjoy the day!

271

Problems cannot be solved by the same level of thinking that created them. (Einstein)

The level of thinking that set your problems in motion to begin with is NOT the level of thinking that may lead you to a solution of those problems.

You must step "out of the box". Take a step back and look at things differently. Why are you seeing this as a problem in the first place? How can this be turned into a situation for goodness? How can YOU change your perception of the situation? What do YOU need to learn from this "misperception"!

Today change your way of thinking- try seeing things differently.

Enjoy the day.

Mary Ellen Ciganovich * www.askmaryellen.com

Words express doing while silence expresses being.

Silence can be a more powerful form of communication than words. Most people in conversation become uncomfortable after a 4 second silence. They have been taught silence is awkward so they fill the air with meaningless words. If you don't know what to say - say nothing. In some situations this is a very wise choice. Music is not music without silence. Think about it - without the rests in music all you have is noise. That is what meaningless conversation (words) is-NOISE!

Today express your beingness - be silent!

Enjoy the day.

Mary Ellen Ciganovich * www.askmaryellen.com

273

By assessing your life rationally instead of emotionally you will open your eyes to your TRUTH.

Situations that seem overwhelming lose their sense of difficulty when your perception changes. Your emotions cloud your perspective. When you look at a situation factually rather than emotionally the degree of difficulty will change. During the holidays it is especially easy to get wrapped up in an emotional whirlwind. Loved ones and family members bring up emotions that dig deep at our heart. Put the past aside- allowing these emotional wounds to heal.

Today take an honest rational look at your life - try to put all emotions aside.

Enjoy the day.

Mary Ellen Ciganovich * www.askmaryellen.com

We are ALL products of the natural world.

At the moment of your birth, you are perfectly in touch with God/Nature/The Universe. As you grow much of the "human experience" is removed and you tend to forget you are a product of the natural world. Your feelings are an authentic response to your natural stimulus. When you discover the sites, sounds, and scents of our synthetic world your memory of nature dies. The strength of your connection to nature revives every time you breathe the fresh air or enjoy the pleasures of organic food.

Today rediscover your place in the Natural World - become one with God I the Universe/ Nature.

Enjoy the day.

Love must always be nurturing and supportive.

Stop looking for love in all the wrong places. Many people are on a journey for love that amounts to trying to stop a "leaky faucet". When you appear to receive love from an outside source it reinforces the societal belief that love is found outside ourselves. This stops "the leak" temporarily. It does not last. True love must always be nurturing and supportive - no strings attached - supportive of both partners – a REAL relationship with no judgements, expectations, motives or assumptions!

Today seek the love you crave inside yourself first. Enjoy the day.

Mary Ellen Ciganovich * www.askmaryellen.com

276

Allow the guidance of your "Higher Self" to take you through your journey with wondrous experiences.

Wonderous experiences and adventures will excite you when you allow your "Higher Self" to lead your journey through life. Trust this power within you to provide valuable information. New possibilities will open up as you step out of your comfort zone. Do not fear making an incorrect decision as when you trust your "Higher Self" this is never a possibility. These nudges from your spiritual center will provide you the "gift of confidence" as you go through bolder explorations.

Today begin an exciting courageous opportunity as you follow your Higher Self.

Enjoy the day.

Mary Ellen Ciganovich * www.askmaryellen.com

By expressing your affection for others openly - your relationships will thrive.

Keep your eyes open for opportunities to spend time with the people you care about. Spend time with them freely and openly without your cell phone or tablet!! Express your feelings speaking in a language your loved ones will understand. You may discover that these people also want to share their feelings with you. Respond with loving gestures and kindnesses. If you have trouble verbalizing feelings put your loving thoughts on paper or make a romantic dinner. Through becoming liberal with your affection to those you love - ensures these individuals understand the depth of your feelings.

Today allow your affection to inspire intimacy. Enjoy the day.

Jealousy is a common human feeling.

Jealousy is a common human feeling and usually stems from a place of lack in your own life. It is a very tough feeling to overcome. There is not a worse feeling than that of life being unfair to us. It is even worse when that someone else is still present in your daily life. This will make it difficult for you to feel and heal your pain. You can normalize your experience by understanding your pain and realizing the fact that jealousy is a common human feeling. Accept and let go!

Today - feel your feelings - sit with the pain - and allow God to help you to let go!

Enjoy the day.

Give of yourself without expectation or acknowledgement.

It is the simple act of doing something - anything - for someone else that can make you feel empowered. It does not matter whether you want to help the homeless or make progress with your own personal goals. The point is you take action. By acting you show the Universe /God that you want to make a difference. Your sense of accomplishment is your reward for any job well done. No thanks needed! Today do something without any expectation of acknowledgement.

Enjoy the day.

280

Your "Dramas" if not controlled or handled correctly can become an addiction.

Your "Dramas" like anything else are a learned habit and can become an addiction. Many of you are accustomed to a certain amount of turmoil in your life. You can make a new choice. To activate this shift in consciousness from "drama" to "peace" become aware of when your dramas arise. Become conscious of how you respond to them. You can access your Higher Power who will assist you in ways you cannot assist yourself.

Today become aware of the dramas that play over and over in your life.

Enjoy the day.

Mary Ellen Ciganovich * www.askmaryellen.com

Regard life as a gift and celebrate what comes to you!

You can always choose to find your "good" right where you stand. You can choose to live in a beautiful home, you can choose to drive a wonderful car and you can choose to be in a right relationship as long as you are content with the home, car or relationship you have right now! This does not mean you should stay in an abusive relationship - of course you should not - and it does not mean you shouldn't strive to have a better life. It means you fully embrace the "here and now".

Regard your life as a gift and celebrate what comes to you. You can still be happy if you do not get your first choice. True bliss (happiness) should run deeper than your immediate need for gratification. People who are happy enjoy giving to others rather than getting for themselves.

Today remember your happiness is not a destination- it is a way of life to be lived day to day.

Enjoy the day!

Mary Ellen Ciganovich * www.askmaryellen.com

282

Patience can bring you a calmness to soothe your emotions and other conflicts.

When you feel quick-tempered you may react strongly when circumstances do not match expectations. Try to be aware of your emotions at all times. Understand what triggers your feelings. Take a few moments to breathe deeply and compose yourself before you approach others or deal with situations. Your emotions are your responsibility and should be dealt with in healthy ways instead of being dumped on others.

Become willing to look past the "heat of the moment" to exercise control and patience.

Today interact well with others as you move through difficult situations.

Enjoy the day.

Mary Ellen Ciganovich * www.askmaryellen.com

Every person must balance their three dimensions of vibratory energy in order to achieve health and peace.

There are (at least) three dimensions of energy vibrating within you. Your mental (mind), the emotional (body), and your spiritual (soul) energies must be balanced to give you peace (health). Do not allow your mind- thoughts- (mental energy) to manipulate your body (emotional energy) and disrupt your spirit (soul energy). Harmonize these energies like a song.

Think your thoughts through - before you feel & interpret them into you body - now intuitively follow your light creating peace and within your soul and balancing all of your vibratory energies.

Today create balance!

Enjoy the day.

Mary Ellen Ciganovich * www.askmaryellen.com

A choice motivated by guilt will not take you where you want to go.

At time we make choices based on trying to please someone else. These choices are usually made out of guilt. Guilt is not loving it comes from a fear based mindset. The Universe/God will never reward a "fear-based" choice. Rewards from The Universe/God are always based on Love! Guilt is a way of controlling a situation (or someone) through fear. This process will NEVER work as you are operating from fear not love!

Today let go of guilt.

Enjoy the day!

We are all learning and teaching together -just in different ways.

We all live in human bodies - we have souls and spirits that are our vehicles as we move through this world. In other words - we are all in the same boat just rowing with different paddles down different rivers. You use many different tools and/or combination of tools to wade through life. We learn differently and at different rates yet the outcome for all of us is eventually the same- love, hope, and joy.

To find these a balanced approach is always best. When you rely on one thing or person too much you will lose your equilibrium and fall off your path into the water with no paddle at all!

Today know you are never alone - just look around you to seek encouragement, motivation and role models.

Enjoy the day.

Mary Ellen Ciganovich * www.askmaryellen.com

286

Be patient with others as this will increase the chances of getting your needs met.

Pause a moment and carefully consider how your choices may be impacting another. Seek to find how you might assist them in their needs. Slow down and become patient when it comes to having your own needs met. Give your time to others and consider how your actions may be affecting them. It is easy - In our society of technology - to feel rushed and pressured. Put aside your haste and connect to people.

Today respond with thoughtfulness and consideration for others.

Enjoy the day.

Mary Ellen Ciganovich * www.askmaryellen.com

Noise is a distraction and can affect you in many ways.

Noise assists you in dealing with uncomfortable thoughts and emotions. Noise distracts you numbing you and preventing you from closure with issues that haunt you. Noise allows you - not to feel - not to heal - avoiding the pain of reality. Let go of this "Veil of noise" that shields you. Go within embracing silence and introspection. Work through your thoughts and emotions allowing the Universe/ God to speak to you.

Today free yourself from the "need for noise".

Enjoy the day.

288

Find encouragement within yourself.

Your "true" inner voice is the one that encourages you, gives you hope and pushes you to believe in yourself. At times you may hear many voices wanting your attention. You are "true" inner voice comes from your knowings - connection to Spirit/God. Your "false" inner voice is connected to Ego - your belief system. A belief always includes a doubt and your knowings are where your truth resides.

Today be quiet and in the silence find your "true" Inner Voice.

Enjoy the day!

Mary Ellen Ciganovich * www.askmaryellen.com

Open your mind to the endless possibilities that exist in our world.

Become hungry for knowledge! Explore the world with a fresh perspective. Feel progressive and become more broad minded than ever before as unique investigate unfamiliar belief systems, ideologies, or philosophical principles. If you are not sure about where to start ask yourself," What do I enjoy doing, learning, reading or studying?" Wisdom does not exist in a vacuum. Open your mind to the myriad possibilities that exist. Do not limit yourself! Explore and experience the wonders of the world through increasing your knowledge base. Make highly informed choices that reflect your awareness of life.

Today accept the fact that you have much to learn- begin your discovery- NOW!

Enjoy the day.

290

Slow down and listen to your natural rhythm.

Everything has a rhythm -day turns to night,
flowers bloom, leaves turn color and drop falling
from the trees. Humans have their own inner
rhythms - tuned to the Universal sense of timing.
Guided by the rising and setting of the sun we
know when to sleep and changes in temperature
tell us what clothes to wear. Our breathing and
heartbeat remind us we are alive - while our minds
and spirits are free to focus on other pursuits.
When you push your body to work beyond its
natural rhythm it diminishes your ability to function
properly. Feeling frantic causes your body to move
faster. You then feel unbalanced. When you move
to your natural rhythm you can achieve all you
need to do with less effort.

Today slow down and listen to your body's natural
rhythm.

Enjoy the day.

Mary Ellen Ciganovich * www.askmaryellen.com

Never be judgmental or defensive - especially in a conversation with a difficult person.

We all encounter a wide variety of people throughout life. Some people touch using in a positive way yet others can be extremely difficult to deal with. Dealing with a difficult person, for a long time can be exhausting. The behavior of this type of person can affect you IF you allow "their stuff' to become part of your baggage. You cannot totally avoid difficult people because through them you will learn your hardest lessons.

The best way to address them is with kindness and loving attitude. You cannot change them -the only person you can change is YOU! Speak to them respectfully, aggressively and with love -letting them know how you feel. Most difficult people won't care how you feel and will not listen to anyone except themselves. Avoid being judgmental or defensive. Learn about yourself and move forward.

Today do not allow a difficult person or situation to have power over you.

Enjoy the day.

Mary Ellen Ciganovich * www.askmaryellen.com

292

Everyone deserves to be given a second chance.

When you meet someone for the first time you create a mind picture of what they are like. You subconsciously determine if that person is worth getting to know. Never be too quick to judge as this may cause you to lose out on an enriching relationship. Always be safe and follow your knowings - (if your knowings telling you to go then go!) First impressions do not always tell the complete picture. Someone might be having a bad day or it might be you who are misjudging them. All of us know from personal experience how painful it is to be misunderstood or judged. Show your good heart today, with no judgements.

Today give someone, especially yourself, a second chance for acceptance and the opportunity for forgiveness.

Enjoy the day and have lots of fun this weekend!

Mary Ellen Ciganovich * www.askmaryellen.com

293

Your natural state of being is to be vibrant, happy and ALIVE!

When you become "worn out" and "run down" you receive what you need from the Universe/God. At times, all of us feel tired and it is during these times we need to slow down and recharge.

Vitamins, healthy eating and rest may restore your physical body to its natural state. Exercise and moving your body will free the toxins needed to move through your body being eliminated. When you feel "run down "take a moment to look at how you are thinking, feeling and acting. You may have too much to deal with and these stressors are overwhelming you draining your energy.

Understand the feeling of being "run down" has less to do with WHAT you are doing and MORE to do with the fact that in your heart you would rather be doing something else!

Today and always listen to your heart- honor it in all situations.

Enjoy the day.

Mary Ellen Ciganovich * www.askmaryellen.com

294

Your human body loves flow and movement.

Your body is not meant to stagnate. Yet, at times you must rest. You can still stretch and move different parts of your body.

When you stretch, your body will become fluid with the rhythm of life. Your mood will lift and you will feel connected with the world around you. By giving your muscles a chance to do what they were created to do you will find other areas of your body benefiting as well. Your mind will be clearer and your fatigue lifted. If you have a job where you walk a lot, then when you exercise- stretch or use hand weights to utilize different muscles. Give yourself the gift of movement!

Today trust your body's ability to move - knowing it has perfect strength and rhythm.

Enjoy the day.

Mary Ellen Ciganovich * www.askmaryellen.com

Consciously release worrisome thoughts and take time to play.

By giving yourself permission to release worrisome thoughts you allow your subconscious mind to continue working on other problems (misperceptions) to provide creative solutions. It is natural to want an immediate resolution and by doing this you might make the situation worse. Take a step back from your "problems" and focus instead on fun.

Give your mind the space it needs to come up with a creative solution. Many times, after enjoying a "fun" activity you have relaxed your mind so much that creative solutions materialize allowing you to come up with a solution.

Today ease your anxiety and play!

Enjoy the day.

Mary Ellen Ciganovich * www.askmaryellen.com

Invite laughter into your life by embracing humor.

A humorous mood can always make the world seem bright. Find reasons to laugh out loud - both at home and at work,especially when you are dealing with challenging circumstances.

When you invite laughter into your life you might find yourself telling jokes or sharing funny stories. Your ability to be happy is yours to control. Within you lies the unique power to choose happiness even when the world seems to be falling apart around you. When you respond to chaos in thus way you are not allowing chaos to rob you of your contentment.

Today lift your spirits with laughter allowing happiness to take its rightful place in your world.

Enjoy the day.

Mary Ellen Ciganovich * www.askmaryellen.com

Allow time for your thoughts to fully form.

A good way to enhance your focus is by slowing your pace allowing time for your thoughts to come, go or stay the course before you choose to act on them. Become observant with a strong awareness of your surroundings. Review each situation carefully taking time to respond not react. As you listen carefully to your thoughts - before acting upon them you can make decisions that benefit your long-term objectives rather than your short-term goals. Impatience is the result of wanting things or situations to be different NOW before you have fully thought through your ideas. As you form these new ideas continue to form detailed action plans. These plans will assist your thoughts to become your reality. Through controlling your thoughts, you will have more opportunities and many more successes!

Today be observant focusing on the full development of your thoughts.

Enjoy the day!

Mary Ellen Ciganovich * www.askmaryellen.com

298

An idealistic attitude can assist you to recognize the potential in people and situations.

You might discount circumstances or people who do not live up to your expectations. Do not discount the many ways they may help you learn about yourself. Learn to look at all the potential blessings that lurk under your disappointments. Adjust your expectations to see the good in others. Adapt to unforeseen circumstances recognizing people are individuals and as such will make mistakes, have judgments, expectations and motives. You can choose to rise above these expectations, judgments and motives to see situations as blessings.

Today focus on the positive nature of people in your life and adjust YOUR attitude.

Enjoy the day.

Mary Ellen Ciganovich * www.askmaryellen.com

Play is a wonderful antidote for the stress and tension in our society.

It is expected, in our society, for you to be diligent, up standing, serious and successful - it can be refreshing to see a person cast off these roles and play! Let go! Take a day, any day, and make it a day you do what you want to do for YOU! Enter a simple world governed only by your heart and soul. Look at the brighter side of life smiling and being a kid again. Project a joyous, optimistic, attitude even if your life seems to be gray. Allow this "Grey cloud" to go- seeing a bright sun reflecting rainbow left behind.

Today feel relaxed and cheerful - cast off your "chains of adulthood" and play.

Enjoy the day.

Do not carry the "weight of the world" upon your shoulders.

Guilt is when you take responsibility for other people's choices and for the type of life those choices attract. This causes you to carry the "weight of the world". The "weight" of all those people whom you want to save and believe you can save. The "weight" of all things you wish were different because their issues trigger things in you that you must work on for yourself! This "weight" you carry on your back is called guilt. Then you wonder why your back hurts or your neck, shoulders or head! You can take responsibility for only two things -

#1 the choices you make in your life and

#2 the way your life is at this moment! Nothing else!

Today cleanse your guilt and give yourself permission to fly.

Enjoy the day.

Mary Ellen Ciganovich * www.askmaryellen.com

301

There is always enough time to accomplish your objectives while still taking care of yourself!

In our society, we are rushed and rushed trying to find time to do more. More of what - more for your family, friends, kids or just a spare moment for yourself? You can find extra "free time" by reassessing your busy schedule. What HAS to be

accomplished? Direct other people to do something that is on your schedule. What can simply be crossed off your list? Do not allow your overloaded series of days and nights to drain your energy. You can always find time to do what you genuinely love to do.

By accessing your schedule, you will find many activities you "think" are important have little to do with your survival or your happiness.

Today regain control by retracting your agenda - find time!

Enjoy your day.

Mary Ellen Ciganovich * www.askmaryellen.com

Learn to praise yourself- and of course- God!

Discover your deep well of confidence and Inner strength by constantly learning to praise the good you see inside of yourself! An easy way to do this is to look at others- as the good you see in others is also inside of you or you would not be able to see it so clearly. You must give yourself credit for being the good person you have become. When others praise you allow this to be a bonus you can freely enjoy. Choose to take responsibility for your own self-worth.

Today focus on strengthening your own sense of validation and confidence - don't forget to praise the Higher power who gave it all to you -God!

Enjoy the day.

Mary Ellen Ciganovich * www.askmaryellen.com

Purpose gives our life meaning.

Almost all humans are born NOT knowing consciously what their "life purpose" is. Discovering this "purpose" will help you to live your life with intention making correct choices that assist you to complete your objectives. Your purpose is unique and will come to fruition as you move through life. Ask yourself, " what do I love to do" or "what us my passion?" Do not worry about the money because when you do what you love to do the money will come!

Today what is your "life purpose?"

Enjoy the day.

Live your dream!

Your dream for your life is inside you. Some people "dream" to be happy. Stop dreaming and simply choose happiness. Listen to the passion within your heart and TAKE ACTION to fulfill your destiny. Be the change you want to see in our world. Live your dream as it is already inside of you waiting to burst forth into fruition. During this time of year as you plan your resolutions for the New Year - chart your course for a new consciousness of expression. The path you choose is your perfect path - do not allow anyone or anything to block your light.

Today wake up and fulfill your dream.

Enjoy the day!

Mary Ellen Ciganovich * www.askmaryellen.com

Going nowhere faster will NOT get you somewhere

Our society keeps going faster and faster. You drive to work in a hurry, you go to lunch and eat as fast as you can, you come home - dinner, homework and other chores must be done in a hurry. You order a computer. It is just about obsolete by the time it arrives at your home. Everyone has to have the fastest cell phone with all the latest features. Technology is growing exponentially. Our society will be impacted and not to our good. Stillness in our society is tantamount to an illusion.

People spin their wheels attempting to accomplish the most in the shortest amount of time with the least amount of effort .

Today slow down and

Enjoy the day!

Mary Ellen Ciganovich * www.askmaryellen.com

306

See the light in yourself in order to bring light into our world.

The " light of the world" dances within you. However, you are unaware of "this light" because you have not looked deep within your own heart.

Reach deep inside yourself and see the colors of light hidden within the darkness. Clear the cobwebs away from this darkness so your light may shine in our society.

Today bring your light to life!

Enjoy the day.

Mary Ellen Ciganovich * www.askmaryellen.com

307

Accept yourself just as you are allowing God to help you become the person you should be.

By accepting yourself just as you are - with no judgments or criticism you take your first step toward becoming everything God wants you to be. Now you may continue walking this path of love assisting with the healing of our planet or you can fall back into your old patterns.

Today accept yourself just the way you are as you help others to accept themselves.

Enjoy the day!

Mary Ellen Ciganovich * www.askmaryellen.com

308

Take responsibility for the life you are living.

You should always take responsibility for the choices you make that complete the life you are living. You should NOT take responsibility for how others feel about your choices. Their feelings are there choices! Never hold others accountable for the choices you make. You cannot fix things for another person and neither can they fix things for you. You CAN listen to them and you can be there for them. When each and every one of accepts responsibility for our own life - it empowers us to create a new pattern and embrace change. In this way - possibly - we can all come together for a better society and world!

Today take responsibility for the way your life is - if there is something you want to change - CHANGE IT!

Enjoy the day.

Look inside yourself to find the place where love begins!

The blocks you have to love - either finding love or loving yourself- lie within you. Inside yourself- inside your own heart -is the place you must first look to dissolve these blocks. All of the blocks you have toward loving yourself (or anyone else) were taught to you by well meaning people. You are now an adult and can choose at any moment to perform your own miracle and remove these blocks. Why are you repeating patterns of negativity, self loathing or judgement of others - when you did not like seeing these patterns as you were growing up. Spread your love around. See with compassion - reach out to help others- become determined to see good. Do it NOW!

Today look inside yourself to find all the love you seek.

Enjoy the day!

Mary Ellen Ciganovich * www.askmaryellen.com

310

Become determined to get things done!

Especially during the busy holiday season - which has just begun- there are tons of tasks taking time away from your daily routine. Give yourself specific goals you can achieve. This will make it easier for you to stay motivated and focused. Even if your to-do list seems overwhelming prioritize your tasks so you can easily see the results.

Today increase your motivational energy and enthusiasm for all the tasks you must do.

Enjoy the day.

311

When you recognize greatness in others - you are seeing the greatness you have inside of you!

We are all moved by greatness when we see it because we know "the feeling" as it resides within each one of us. The achievements of any one person belong to many as we accomplish nothing by ourselves. We have been guided, nurtured, encouraged and supported by the society we live in. Greatness is simply being the best you can be - the best our world has to offer.

Today trust in yourself- become inspired - have courage to embrace YOUR greatness!

Enjoy the day.

Mary Ellen Ciganovich * www.askmaryellen.com

Motivate yourself through blessing the fruits of all your hard work.

During most of your day there are always things that will bring you down causing you to lose focus. Know there is always an end to any task you do not like. By remembering to stay on track, you can get through these down times. When you have faith, you will be carried through these down moments staying inspired and motivated. Consider your underlying fears surrounding the tasks you dislike. Now imagine these duties already accomplished. Feeling this sense of accomplishment - beforehand - will make it easier for you to stay focused and finish.

Today stay more deeply motivated and committed to your work.

Enjoy the day.

Mary Ellen Ciganovich * www.askmaryellen.com

313

When you accept everything, you have been given there will be excitement in all areas of your life!

Feelings of agitation reflect your internal impatience with your life. Learning to accept things as they are will allow your mind to guide you toward aspects of your life that excite you. Should feelings of boredom arise - take a few minutes to be still and observe your surroundings. Take a breath- as you breathe mentally say to yourself, "I accept my life as it is." Focus on the things in your life that are valuable and add meaning to your existence. Allow yourself to see the Wonders that are already present in your life. Accept everything you have been given with an excitement for living!

Today become aware of what you have - then you will come to understand how complete your life really is.

Enjoy the day.

Mary Ellen Ciganovich * www.askmaryellen.com

Choose a way to Love- Unconditionally!

The way you choose to love is unique to every individual. Depending on how you were raised - you formed a "mental picture" of what love is and another picture of how to give love to someone else. Being single or in a relationship are both good options for living a full life and one is not better than the other. Choosing to be single is a wonderfully beautiful way to take time discovering yourself. Choosing to have a mate gives you an opportunity to see yourself through another person's eyes. What is right for you is not necessarily right for another. Do not judge.

Today embrace life fully - whether on your own or with a mate.

Enjoy the day.

Mary Ellen Ciganovich * www.askmaryellen.com

315

Keep strong boundaries between work and personal relationships.

When you blur the lines between business and personal relationships you may become disappointed. Figure out why you may want to tum a professional relationship into a personal one. When you keep boundaries between work and play you will be able to focus your energies without crossing into territory that may cost you a job or marriage. I am sure there are cases of balance when lines are crossed- however this is a difficult choice and - in my opinion - is not a good idea for either person involved.

Ask yourself: What are your motives for crossing the boundaries? What expectations do you have of the relationship? When these questions cannot be answered peacefully- DO NOT cross the lines!

Today know what your boundaries or should be. Enjoy the day.

316

Take time to assess the effect of your choices.

An upbeat outlook and proactive attitude can attract several positive opportunities into your life. The temptation to jump into new opportunities and or new relationships may be overwhelming - however - before you jump slow down to clearly see your choices. What impact will these new choices have on your life? How might this change your future? Will this put you on your right path or might it "kick" you in a wrong direction? Take a moment or two to make the most of your opportunities allowing yourself to weigh all your options. What are your knowings telling you. Be quiet sit with God and listen!

Today slow down and become willing to make the choices that will truly benefit your life!

Enjoy the day.

Mary Ellen Ciganovich * www.askmaryellen.com

Perfect your ability to not only feel your "knowings" and to follow your "knowings."

We cannot see God (except in His creations) yet we can feel His wisdom surrounding us. You can ask Him questions - we all do - mostly in the form of prayers and we all receive His answers.

The secret is in the ability to be quietly intuitive. Even more important is your ability to know you have this connectedness with God. You must have the ability to feel and know what you feel. How can God know the answer to a question you are fumbling with asking? God gives us everything we asked for- sometimes it is just in another form. Place your thoughts in a drawer (figure of speech)- put your ego to sleep- sit comfortably, breathe slowly and be with God. Now ask your questions - feel your feelings and know God is with you.

Today feel your wisdom- allowing it to connect with God – know God and you will know yourself. Enjoy the day.

Mary Ellen Ciganovich * www.askmaryellen.com

The "present" is a pleasure to live in when you keep your expectations in check.

Future thoughts prevent you from enjoying the "present moment". Your expectations bring up worries, stripping the joy of NOW. Your energy is better spent simply deriving as much enjoyment as possible from your life in this "present moment". Excitement, suspense and fears of the future can overstimulate you leaving you unable to focus on what is occurring around you. There is nothing wrong with expecting situations or others to turn out the way you want- it is only when you get swept away in these expectations that you will find:

1. Either people do not live up to them - so you become depressed ruining the "present moment" or

2. You stress yourself out with too many expectations of yourself- again you become depressed ruining the "present moment".

Today live in the "Present Moment!

Enjoy the day.

Mary Ellen Ciganovich * www.askmaryellen.com

Take time every day to quiet your mind.

At times decisions are difficult to make because you are interrupted by so many unwanted thoughts. This can leave you feeling overwrought, uncomfortable and anxious regarding your ability to make choices. You can return yourself to balance by quieting your mind. There are many ways to go about this process:

1. Meditating

2. Journaling

3. Deep breathing techniques

4. Walking in nature- beach, forest, woods or any type of soothing garden.

5. Beginning or doing a hobby that soothes you - photography, cooking, scrapbooking, knitting, sewing and there are many more examples.

By doing any of these your unwanted thoughts will disappear as you ease yourself into a state of calmness. Today use relaxation techniques to quiet your mind and improve your focus.

Enjoy the day.

Mary Ellen Ciganovich * www.askmaryellen.com

By empowering others, you empower yourself!

One of the best ways to help others is by instilling in other people are sense of empowerment and courage. Rather than taking on their problems and trying to solve them - simply ask yourself which words and/or phrases could you say to make them feel inspired. Then allow them to courageously tackle their issues. You can inspire a person with your words, verbally expressing your belief in them or in written form with a heartfelt note or email. Because the Universe/God reflects to us the quality of the energy we put forth - you will benefit from your efforts to build up other people. You will feel empowered about taking on your own misperceptions (problems).

Today make this a day where you recognize the strengths you see in others - be sure to tell them!!

Enjoy the day.

Mary Ellen Ciganovich * www.askmaryellen.com

321

When you indulge in self-pity you only make a bad day worse.

When you think, you are an innocent victim of a dismal fate you are seeing your life through inaccurate lenses. The thoughts running through your mind are NOT helpful and will NOT change your circumstances. Feel these uncomfortable feelings - process them and let them go. You might want to write about these feelings, then shred or burn your letter. Plan to get back on your feet.

Today release unpleasant experiences and negative emotions.

Enjoy the day.

Mary Ellen Ciganovich * www.askmaryellen.com

Face your Truth to keep your life moving in a forward direction.

Facing a "Truth" about yourself is always uncomfortable. It might be a small truth- like not wanting to do a chore around the house or a large truth such as not being able to see your negative qualities. Most of the time your Truth is evident- starring you right in the face. You see it in other people to save yourself- your ego- from facing this truth in yourself. Truth, about yourself, will always make you feel uncomfortable.

Today accept the fact - there is no way to avoid Truth!

Enjoy the day.

Mary Ellen Ciganovich * www.askmaryellen.com

323

Remain calm anchored in the peace within your soul.

Your emotional connections to your family, relationships, work etc... can leave you feeling

moody especially during this time of year. When you remain calm anchored in the peace within your soul - you can support each other with a clear mind. It is natural to have a sense of empathy when you care about someone yet we must always remember these people are reacting to their own frustrations! Respond back with a loving attitude - standing in Truth and peace. In this way whatever you are confronting will not escalate.

Today allow your loved ones to experience their emotions - show them empathy and a loving response.

Enjoy the day.

Mary Ellen Ciganovich * www.askmaryellen.com

When something you are doing isn't working for you in your life - doing more of it will not work either!

This is the definition of insanity - doing the same thing over and over again while expecting different results. During this time of year many of you have family members visiting or you might be visiting them. When these people "push your buttons" irritating you - try something different. Respond out of "love" (kindness) instead of reacting out of that old "fear" picture you have replayed in the past. Try humor, compassion and understanding to have a different result. Understand that at that moment they are doing the very best they can do.

Today show them the love and respect you would like to receive from them.

Enjoy the day - and know I am very thankful for all of you!

Mary Ellen Ciganovich * www.askmaryellen.com

325

The only gifts worth having are those that increase when you give them. (ACIM)

Kindness, compassion, understanding, laughter, and forgiveness do not lose there value when you give them. On the contrary, they increase in value and expand outward. Both the giver and the receiver gain. Gifts of money or material objects are gifts leaving someone indebted to another. On this Thanksgiving day - while you are visiting with friends and family - give a gift that will result in everyone winning!

Today and throughout this holiday season give a gift that will last forever!

Empower yourself to shine your unique light upon the world - transcend your limitations.

Not everyone will like you -that is okay- do not take it personally. You must to release the need for other people's approval. While approval from other's is a great feeling, you may lose your way on your own path if you depend on someone else's approval. When someone else does not like you -it is NOT about you. It is because they see something in you that reminds them of the part of themselves they do not like. The best you can do is to follow your own inner guidance with as much integrity as possible.

Today empower yourself to shine your unique light- fully and freely upon our world.

Enjoy the day!

Mary Ellen Ciganovich * www.askmaryellen.com

When you see anything as a "failure" you lose the ability to see Truth.

In our society, the word "failure" has a very negative connotation. Just say the word failure and see how it makes you feel. It probably takes you back to your childhood where you first heard the word. You are never a failure when you learn something. I encourage you to throw the word failure out of your vocabulary. Take time, in every situation, to see things differently. What have you learned from this "failure" situation? If your answer is nothing you are doomed to repeat this again until you do learn your life lesson.

Today know you are a student of life and NEVER A FAILURE!

Enjoy the day.

Mary Ellen Ciganovich * www.askmaryellen.com

Recognize the abundance you have in your life -
see there is nothing you lack.

During this time of year be sure to recognize the
abundance you have in your life. It is human nature
to always strive for more and you do not need
more! When we become focused on more we tend
to hoard our resources viewing our life through
eyes of what we "don't" have. Turn your thoughts
toward being blessed today as you realize how rich
you are!

Today recognize your abundance - practice
gratitude!

Enjoy the day!

329

Break the cycle of negative thoughts and limitations that run through your mind.

Negative thoughts and limitations are simply habits you have picked up through the years. You are mimicking a habit you grew up around - whether from relatives or society in general. You did not like to be around these habits when you were younger yet even today you nurture these negative thoughts. When others continue this behavior you usually judge and condemn their behavior. You have a choice to break this negative thought pattern and teach your children differently.

Today make a choice to rid yourself of negative thought patterns and limitations.

Enjoy the day.

Mary Ellen Ciganovich * www.askmaryellen.com

Become receptive to intimacy.

Express a desire to know your friends and loved ones in deeper ways. People often believe you know everything there is to know about your friends, family and loved ones. Often this is not the case. Ask questions being supportive of their lives. Express a genuine interest in them. Give them the opportunity to share. You might begin to see this person in a. new light - creating a deeper level of intimacy in your relationship remember to listen to their answers without interrupting with your own stories!

Intimacy is when YOU allow someone else to see into you! In -to - Me - See= intimacy!

Today consciously connect with someone around you - family member or friend - allow them to see into you while you have an opportunity to see the beautiful person they are.

Enjoy the day!

Mary Ellen Ciganovich * www.askmaryellen.com

Curb your busy-ness by focusing primarily on the duties that are significant.

Especially during the holidays life can become horribly hectic. Many obligations make you frantic and as a result a rude or inconsiderate comment may be said. Realize your natural human limitations while you take a deep breath to ease your impatience. Finding inner peace can be easy when you accept that your life will unfold at its own pace. Prioritize your schedule while you appreciate life's journey for what it is - the fulfillment of your purpose.

Today look at your schedule, duties and goals to prioritize what is important.

Enjoy the day.

Honesty creates Harmony.

When you are truthful in your relationships, and interactions - your life will flow peacefully. Problems or misperceptions arise when you are not honest with yourself or others. The more open you are - the more receptive your loved ones become to you. Speak your truth - gently and compassionately - from your heart. This opens the way for an honest exchange of thoughts and ideas.

Today communicate with understanding and love

creating honesty and harmony.

Enjoy the day.

333

Instead of struggling against the "current of life" use the natural flow of life like a mighty wind.

Trust the Universe/God is taking you exactly where you need to be in every situation. Instead of struggling against the "current of life" have faith and allow this current to carry you through your tough times. Become willing to let go of your resistance and your control. Make choices to become exhilarated by life as you effortlessly ride this current!

Today allow your soul to soar with freedom as you flow with the universe God.

Enjoy the day.

Mary Ellen Ciganovich * www.askmaryellen.com

To create peace in your life, soften what is rigid in your heart.

All of us have places in our hearts we have shut down due to the hurts we have experienced in our lives. In order to create your peace, you must soften these places that are rigid in your heart. Forgive yourself for holding on to these hurts. Forgive others! By holding these hurts in your heart - the only person you hurt is YOU. The other person- probably- has no idea they even hurt you or maybe they do not even care. Find creative ways to serve others with your talents and skills as this will allow those places in your heart to heal.

Today begin softening what is rigid in your heart through becoming AWARE of these rigid places and forgiving yourself!

Enjoy the day.

Mary Ellen Ciganovich * www.askmaryellen.com

Love is like a crown of thorns worn by two people who master in the art of forgiveness.

Forgiveness is heart medicine. It involves a healing experience between you and God. Through forgiveness you learn that God's most powerful force is love. When two people are in a relationship this "art of forgiveness" should be practiced daily.

The forgiveness I speak of is the "inner work" you do to increase your experience of freedom. This "inner work" of forgiveness is not to fix yourself. It is to love yourself just the way you are so your partner can mirror that love back to you. The blessing of forgiveness releases all your isolation, fear and pain bringing you closer to God.

Today begin learning the "art of forgiveness" by forgiving yourself.

Enjoy the day.

Mary Ellen Ciganovich * www.askmaryellen.com

Rejection is not failure -failure is giving up - rejection is simply God's way of showing you a different path.

Rejection is not bad. How you choose to handle it can lead to failure or by choosing a new path - rejection may lead to a great success. Use your imagination to integrate your creative thinking potential seeing others' ways to promote yourself or your product. Your ability to pursue long-term goals is heightened with determination after you face a rejection.

Today take time to visualize your thoughts using any rejection as a stepping-stone for success.

Enjoy the day.

Mary Ellen Ciganovich * www.askmaryellen.com

337

Express yourself from your heart by connecting with others on an emotional level.

Become inclined to express yourself from your heart rather than your head. When you speak from your heart it allows you to express how you truly feel. Your "heart conversation" directly channel what is in your soul. Even when you interact with others speaking from the heart allows you to show a higher level of compassion. Intimacy happens when you allow others to see into you as you truly are. This authentic expression is a key to intimacy.

Today feel the richness and beauty that comes from expressing yourself from your heart.

Enjoy the day.

Mary Ellen Ciganovich * www.askmaryellen.com

Discovering who you are apart from your "roles" in life takes time and courage.

Your identity is an elusive concept because with time it changes. Your "role in life" is a small selection of traits that represent your sense of self. In Truth, you are beings of light. Pure energy that inhabits physical bodies striving to learn your earthly lessons. Your true self exists whether you are at work, retired, whether you are married or divorced or are a mother, father, friend, etc.... (whatever your identity label is). You may find it difficult to separate these labels to your "true" identity because you have denied your authentic self for a long time.

Today develop your "sense of self' as a being of light.

Enjoy the day.

Mary Ellen Ciganovich * www.askmaryellen.com

339

Express your enthusiasm for life every day!!

Go outside today- participate in activities that require you to exert yourself physically. This physical activity will make you feel healthy and energized. Take a brisk walk or spend time at a gym. Expressing enthusiasm for life through physical activity is a natural way to increase your energy levels. Many times, people respond to exhaustion or mental tension by becoming sedentary. I know it seems odd to counter fatigue through exercise yet when you engage in physical activities you are challenging your body. Your body then responds by pumping oxygen through your body freeing toxins leaving you feeling energized.

Today enhance your energy levels by participating in vigorous physical activity.

Enjoy the day

340

Stay true to your Truth while being considerate of other people's values.

You can always express your truths openly to others while respecting their beliefs. Even though they may differ from your own beliefs you should be respectful and listen attentively. Speak your mind calmly and thoughtfully when you respond. When you respect other people's beliefs they will become considerate of yours. You should never have a need to defend your beliefs as that leads to a self-righteous combative attitude. Remember Truth never has to be defended!

Today become willing to openly listen to someone else's point of view.

Enjoy the day.

Mary Ellen Ciganovich * www.askmaryellen.com

341

Friends give us the gift of learning about ourselves.

Friends enrich our lives in so many ways. They offer you opportunities to know yourself through your similarities and differences. Friends act as mirrors sending back to us those characteristics in ourselves that we love AND characteristics in ourselves we need to change. Be open to learning about friendships - good or bad. A good friend will assist you in finding your path as you walk through life together.

Today be grateful for all your friends and remember to have a friend you must be a friend.

Enjoy the day.

Mary Ellen Ciganovich * www.askmaryellen.com

342

Question your compulsion to constantly give your children things.

Especially during this time of year we tend to inundate our children with things they do not need. This comes either from our own desire to create a feeling of abundance or from a need to be "liked" by society -children -friends etc..

Both of these motives are not conscious and they stem from unresolved issues from our own childhood. Be aware of this Truth and see what your children really need - your time, your attention - or just good memories made with you.

Today make sure your children are being provided with a safe secure and loving childhood.

Enjoy the day.

Mary Ellen Ciganovich * www.askmaryellen.com

343

The message of pain is all about healing.

When you feel pain your first impulse is often to use it with medication. You forget that pain is the body's way of letting you know- that it- your body, spirit or mind need attention. A sore throat might inform you to rest your voice while a headache my address hunger or stressed. Respond to these messages by looking at the underlying meaning behind where the pain is radiating from in your body. Emotional pain, another type of pain, can also provide you with valuable information. Take a few deep breaths and quietly sit with the pain. Allow it to speak to you and providing healing.

Today decode your pain messages.

Enjoy the day.

Mary Ellen Ciganovich * www.askmaryellen.com

344

If you want to be young -act young!

The easiest way to promote youth within yourself is to behave in a youthful light-hearted manner. Too many times we as adults "think" we must adopt an attitude of sternness to promote maturity. A childlike mindset will help you to see the challenges in front of you in a new light. When you play, you remind yourself of the importance of fun even in the responsible world of being an adult. Being reminded of fun can make you feel more youthful and energetic.

Today become inspired to be light-hearted and imaginative. Enjoy the day.

Mary Ellen Ciganovich * www.askmaryellen.com

345

Create your own miracle through "Awareness of Self',

Miracles do not have to be big supernatural events. Miracles can happen at any time to anyone when you choose to see things differently. When you stop judging people - that is a miracle. When you change your perception about any situation, person, diagnosis etc... then you have created your own miracle. You have performed an action that contradicts known scientific principles. That is the definition of a miracle!

Today become aware of yourself and perform your own miracle.

Enjoy the day.

Mary Ellen Ciganovich * www.askmaryellen.com

346

Create stronger bonds through positive experiences with the people you love.

Reconnecting with relatives and or friends you have not seen in a while creates a foundation for another shared memory. These recollections will sustain you while you are apart from one another. Take time to really enjoy yourself with your loved ones- remembering pleasant memories from the past. Your laughter and socialization will bring you closer together.

Today create new memories and enjoy the company of your loved ones.

Enjoy the day.

Heighten your awareness of your environment and the people around you.

When you feel a sense of uncertainty or uneasiness it is an indicator that something about your environment (or the people around you) need your attention! Do not simply write off these suspicions take a moment to become aware of everything going on around you. If you still feel uneasy -leave! It is much better to be safe than sorry as the adage goes. These feelings of uncertainty empower you to determine and deal with any trouble that might be heading your way.

Today still all anxieties through positive action. Enjoy the day.

Mary Ellen Ciganovich * www.askmaryellen.com

348

Your life and the world is all A MATTER OF FAITH!

Without faith, the world would seem like a dangerous, unpredictable place. Choose to trust and have faith that goes beyond any human comprehension level. When you trust in your actions - you will find a positive shift in your life. People around you will show a level of compassion that reflects the faith you are showing to them. These small kindnesses have wide-ranging consequences toward the goodness of humanity in general. This faith provided through your trust will spread like ripples in water touching the lives of individuals who go beyond your sphere of influence.

Today have faith and spread trust.

Enjoy the day.

Mary Ellen Ciganovich * www.askmaryellen.com

349

Your life matters and you are important!

Every single person matters! Your very existence affects countless people in many ways. We are each a microcosm of a larger universe. The world simply could not exist, as it is now, if you or any one of us were not in it. On some level, you may believe your life does not matter. This may come from a self rejecting or belittling believe you formed as a child to be safe. You are now an adult and can reform these falsehoods. These beliefs, of your own unimportance, limit you.

Today shift your perceptions - know your life matters - a lot!

Enjoy the day.

Mary Ellen Ciganovich * www.askmaryellen.com

350

The opinions of others are merely "their thoughts".

Accept this fact- the opinions of others are merely their thoughts -do NOT regard them as your truth. Learning to accept people's opinions as simply their perceptions can help you avoid stress and family disagreements. When you believe everything, other people say you feel vulnerable. Do not take what they say personally - allow them to have different reasons for their own viewpoint.

Today allow other people to have their thoughts as they allow you to have yours.

Enjoy the day.

Mary Ellen Ciganovich * www.askmaryellen.com

View an ending (or a loss) as an opportunity for a new beginning.

A significant ending in your life can leave you feeling alone, unsure and even depressed. You may experience a sense of loss or feel sad because a phase of your life has ended. Find solace in the fact that all beginnings are first preceded by endings. While you mourn for the past look forward toward an even better future. Allow your past to be left behind for an entire wealth of opportunities to come forward. Letting go of "what was" will assist you to focus on the pleasures that are coming into your life. Endings are just transitional periods - preparing you for an even better future.

Today begin at the starting point for the next amazing phase of your life journey!

Enjoy the day.

Consciously focus on the positive (real) side of any situation.

By allowing small frustrations to roll off your shoulders you will create the ability to enjoy yourself on any occasion. You can take this ability to the next level by "choosing" to see the positive side of any situation. When you encounter conflicts or difficulties make an effort to pause and ask yourself," how can I see things differently"? Recognize these positive (real) things you can learn about yourself from navigating the situation smoothly.

Today do not become caught up in the negative side of any situation.

Enjoy the day.

353

The key to living a life full of love is to accept and allow.

Accept yourself with all your human flaws. Allow yourself - give yourself permission - to love yourself. (especially with these flaws) These flaws make you unique and special! Be compassionate with yourself and others, knowing they need encouragement just as you do. Become grateful for everything in your life by spending a few moments each day thanking God for His goodness. Show appreciation to the Universe by doing things for others or giving of your time and talents. Risk being vulnerable to have true intimacy with another. Finally, practice the art of receiving as this is just as important as giving.

Today accept and allow.

Enjoy the day.

354

To know the difference between fear and courage
is to believe anything is possible.

It has been said that the definition of courage is
knowing something is difficult and doing it anyway.
Begin your shift out of fear towards love by telling
yourself and KNOWING anything is possible.
Connect with other people of your "like mind-set"
to support you through this life process. When you
open your heart and mind - especially joining with
others' - you will discover anything is possible.

Today know you can face adversity with dignity and
integrity.

Enjoy the day.

Mary Ellen Ciganovich * www.askmaryellen.com

355

Freedom is the opportunity to do what you want when you want and the ability to choose how you want to do it.

No matter where you were born, at the time of your birth, you were free and innocent. Sometimes due to geography and politics, your freedoms are controlled. Even people in America who "think" they are free are not free if they allow their fears to control them. This ability to "think your own thoughts" and "make your own choices" is precious. The price for freedom is high! Many people all over the world have laid down their lives to pursue freedom for their country and the people who live there.

Today express gratitude for all the freedoms you have been given.

Enjoy the day!

Mary Ellen Ciganovich * www.askmaryellen.com

356

Free yourself from self-sabotage.

When you are not moving in the right direction in your life, you can be certain you are repeating an old "life pattern" of self- sabotage.- When you are aware and understand the patterns of self-sabotage you are using on yourself- you can then "free yourself' from these patterns. (if you choose to!!!) Allow yourself to interact in the world with a greater sense of success, joy and fulfillment. To do this, you must -first- face your fear, anger, negativity and other difficult emotions. Leading you to step fully into the greatest expression of yourself.

Today find wisdom within your old wounds - allowing these wounds to finally heal.

Enjoy the day.

Mary Ellen Ciganovich * www.askmaryellen.com

357

Escape from your daily routine!

It is easy to get caught up in the demands of "home life" because there are ALWAYS things to do or fix. Set some boundaries and assign tasks to other family members - otherwise you will probably feel drained or out of balance. Be sure to integrate self-care into your daily schedule. Turn yourself "off "for 5 minutes, 30 minutes, or even an hour every day.

Today take care of yourself!

Enjoy the day.

Mary Ellen Ciganovich * www.askmaryellen.com

358

Enjoy the age you are NOW!

Every age provides unique experiences and insights. Do not wish your life away. By doing this you are denying the joys every year of wisdom brings to you. Take pleasure and appreciate every milestone you reach. Discover the sense of freedom you create with each year. Enjoy all of the "life memories" you have created.

Today embrace and love the age you are NOW! Enjoy the day.

Contentment is never in the future because the future is NOW.

You can be content at any point in time - simply choose it. Especially during this time of year it may be difficult to find contentment. The family is here -

kids are running around - presents are strewn all over the room- and dinner is either overcooked or late. Yes, turmoil happen - yet you can still find contentment by simply choosing to stay in a loving place.

Today and especially during this holiday season choose contentment- Christ would want you to! Have a very special and joyful holiday season!

Mary Ellen Ciganovich * www.askmaryellen.com

When you approach the world with a positive (R.E.A.L.*) attitude- an abundant supply of blessings is a natural result.

By feeling competent with your ability to deal with the world you will attract new people and experiences into your life. Your positive (R.E.A.L*.)energy will attract better into your life then you can imagine. No matter what the moods of the people around you are the Universe/God will reflect back to you all the energy you are radiating. When you are a confident you are rewarded with goodness sure to come.

Today approach the world with a positive (R.E.A.L*) attitude to ensure many good blessings as a natural result.

Enjoy the day.

*Really Enthusiastic About Life

Mary Ellen Ciganovich * www.askmaryellen.com

As a co-creator with the Universe/God you can only plan and control so much!

When you feel busy running from one appointment to another be comforted by the fact that you are being productive. Energy levels will eb and flow like the tides of the ocean. Make the most of your "high energy" time by accomplishing what is important. Allow yourself to rest preparing for the next "flow of energy". Keep balance while working with the Universe/God to complete the tasks you are presented.

Today enjoy accomplishing more with your energy while you intersperse your tasks with a well-deserved rest.

Enjoy the day.

Mary Ellen Ciganovich * www.askmaryellen.com

Become grounded - choose not to get caught up in thus fast paced world.

Live simply with more time to enjoy just being alive. Become in touch with your soul - know what you like and dislike. Build your foundation on your "sense of self". Be sure to assist, support, teach or help others. See all of the beauty that surrounds you in this Universe and appreciate it! Value your friends and family by becoming a source of support for them. Move your body! Physical exercise is important to your mind, body and soul. Put aside time to be quiet for in the stillness resides your peace.

Today ground yourself that take some quiet time for yourself!

Enjoy the day.

Mary Ellen Ciganovich * www.askmaryellen.com

363

No matter how dark the moment Love and Hope are always present.

It is when we go through our dark moments that we learn the most about ourselves. As you go through these "dark moments" cling to the love and hope your friends/family offer to you. See this "loving light" pulling you out of the darkness into the light that lies in front of you. Visualize yourself seeing in the dark situation differently Find your inner strength through your connection to God or your Higher Power.

Today no matter what you are going through know that love and hope are always with you!

Enjoy the day.

Mary Ellen Ciganovich * www.askmaryellen.com

364

Never look back- always look forward- staying in touch with each and every NOW moment.

Quit kicking yourself for something you did in the past. Allow it to stay there - in the past. You cannot undo it - you cannot fix it - simply learn from it and go forward. If an apology is necessary make sure you contact the person and apologize for whatever action you "think" was incorrect. Always look forward to smell the fresh air, take time to look at every full moon, the stars or even the clouds. Take a walk in the city and listen to the beautiful city noises instead of complaining about them. Use all of your senses to see, here, taste and touch the beautiful experiences you have materializing in the moments of your life.

Today and as we come upon a New Year leave the past behind!

Enjoy the day.

Mary Ellen Ciganovich * www.askmaryellen.com

365

The choices you make reveal the true nature of your character.

It is important to make correct choices. Especially on this night New Year's Eve, you might find yourself in a situation where you have to make a difficult decision. Stop - ask yourself," what is the RIGHT thing to do." Now act upon this "good" decision. During theses times your true character will be tested. Do not allow one night to determine the rest of your life.

Today and always make good choices!

Enjoy the day!

Mary Ellen Ciganovich * www.askmaryellen.com

Where there is a beginning -there is also an ending!

Everything is always okay in the end- if it is not- then it must NOT be the end! This statement of truth defines why worry is unnecessary. Situations always turn out exactly the way they are supposed to -for better or for worse. Just because you are "seeing" a situation as being "the worst thing ever"- in the long run it may turn out to put you in another situation that will fulfill your true potential.

Worrying about anything does not fix it or make it better. It might give you a headache or a stomach ulcer or etc.... Worrying is a societal teaching that should be discarded. If you are thinking to yourself this," situation will never end," - you have a choice - end it where it is or stick with it until you have the results you want.

Today make a choice to move forward with your next step.

Enjoy the day.

Mary Ellen Ciganovich * www.askmaryellen.com

"Truth" the book has, as all things must, come to an end. Will there be a second? I do not know, I suppose that is up to you "the reader".

If you enjoyed my book, "Truth", please tell your friends. I welcome any personal notes you might wish to send.

I will continue to post a "Truth of the day" on Facebook, Twitter, LinkedIn, Instagram and other social media sites. I welcome you to follow these posts if you desire.

Facebook- Mary Ellen Ciganovich

Twitter- @askmaryellen

Instagram- maryciganovich LinkedIn- Mary Ellen Ciganovich www.askmaryellen.com

Sincerely with love, Mary Ellen Ciganovich askmaryellen@aol.com

Mary Ellen Ciganovich is the award-winning author of," Healing Words, Life Lessons to Inspire", which debuted in 2011. She is responsible for posting a "Truth of the day" on Facebook, Twitter, Instagram, LinkedIn, Pinterest, and Tumblr. This book of 366 Truths is a result of those posts.

Mary Ellen grew up in a suburb of Atlanta, Georgia and attended the University of Georgia graduating Magna Cum Laude in Education. She went on to teach middle school and is responsible for building 2 Nature Trails that are still in existence today. Mary Ellen wrote her first book on environmental activities that could be utilized on these trails.

Even before attending college, Mary Ellen was on a spiritual path to conquer her own diagnosis'. While in first grade, she was diagnosed with Petite Mal Temporal Lobe epilepsy. Her family took this diagnosis with tremendous disapproval, making Mary Ellen's self-esteem plummet. Mary Ellen turned to God with prayers, love and at times anger looking for answers. While going to the University of Georgia she found some through being a member of the Alpha Chi Omega sorority. Her sisters accepted her unconditionally while her own family had not!

Mary Ellen Ciganovich * www.askmaryellen.com

Mary Ellen married her first husband in 1975 and had a daughter, Stephanie in 1977. When this marriage ended, Mary Ellen moved back to Atlanta, Georgia and took up racquetball to positively deal with her anger. In 1989, Mary Ellen was a ranked racquetball player although this did not last for long. During the finals of a State match she lost vision and had to end the match-forfeiting the match to her opponent. After going to an eye doctor, her internist then her neurologist, she was told she had Multiple Sclerosis.

Not one to panic, Mary Ellen began to learn about MS- what exactly is it and how could it be handled holistically since at the time there were no MS treatments. So far with very few medications, Mary Ellen handles her case of MS using God (prayers), herbs, meditation, a strict diet and A LOT of exercise.

The Truths that she writes about daily and in this book, help her to fight the MS Monster keeping "it" in its cave! Today Mary Ellen has been happily married to her husband for over 20 years. She and her husband Peter reside outside Chattanooga, TN.

Mary Ellen Ciganovich * www.askmaryellen.com

Bibliography

The Holy Bible, KJ Version, Collins World publishers, (Romans 12:2- quoted in Truth 111) (Psalm 46- quoted in Truth 158) (Exodus- quoted in Truth 158) (1ST Corinthians- quoted in Truth 81)

A Course in Miracles, Foundation for Inner Peace, 1996, second edition, (quoted in Truth 49)

Brown, H. Jackson, Jr., Author of Life's Little Instruction Book, (quoted in Truth 83)

Christ, Jesus,- Truth Teacher- Son of God, (quoted in Truth 117)

Plato, Greek Philosopher, teacher, (quoted in Truth 104)

Socrates, philosopher, teacher, ancient Greek writer, (quoted in Truth 68)

Stephenson, Drew, Actor, www.itsdrewstephenson.com (quoted in Truth 81)

Winfrey, Oprah, producer, author, publisher, actress, TV personality (quoted in Truth 3)

Mary Ellen Ciganovich * www.askmaryellen.com